UNFINISHED BUSINESS...

First published by **The Class War Federation**
and **A.K. Press**, in May 1992.

Printed and bound in the U.K.

Trade distribution;
A.K. Distribution, 3, Balmoral Place, Stirling,
Scotland, F K 8 2 R D.

British Library Cataloguing in Publication Data
Class War Federation
Unfinished Business :
Politics of the Class War Federation.
I. Title
322 . 4

ISBN 1- 873176 - 45 - 7

Dedication;

**This book is dedicated
to all those class warriors
who are fighting for a better world,
especially our comrade and friend
Ken Keating.**

Contents

Contents

About this book

This book represents in broad terms the ideas that the Class War Federation has come to agreement on up to the present time - Spring 1992. As in the many other aspects of the Federation's activities the manner of the production of this book is the direct opposite of what you would find in a left-wing party.

A group of editors were given the task of assembling the Federation's records from conferences, weekend schools, articles in *Class War*, the *Heavy Stuff* etc. Their brief was to work towards a clear and straightforward statement of what we believe in. As we worked on this we received contributions from within and without the Federation, including some disaffected ex-members of various left-wing parties.

The first version of this book was then circulated throughout the Federation and elsewhere. This was then followed by a debate at a national conference to discuss, criticise and decide on changes to this first version. Alterations, both specific and general, were discussed and decided upon there and people volunteered to rewrite sections in accordance with conference decisions. Next the re-written and re-edited text was again circulated around the Federation for comment and criticism. A second conference was held to agree final alterations and it was then accepted as the first in-depth statement of the ideas and politics of the Class War Federation.

At this point you might expect us to claim, like a left-wing party, that this book contains all the answers needed by those who want to destroy capitalism and the State and build a new society.

But we don't, that would be the height of arrogance and stupidity. However, we feel we can claim that this book contains much of what the Left and the anarchists have forgotten or retreated from. We see this book as being a much needed breath of fresh air that gives a useful and relevant interpretation to the honourable tradition of working class resistance to oppression.

Importantly you the reader should view this book as being part of a wider debate that is at present going on within the working class about changing the society that we at present find ourselves forced to live in.

Here you will find a survey of our present situation and how we arrived here, together with the Federations analysis of recent history, finally we give an outline of what we think is required to bring about change.

This book is not intended to be taken as a blueprint for revolution. It is meant to be used as a tool to help you understand the world we live in and come to some clear conclusions about it.

In putting this book together the emphasis has been on clarity, we have used everyday language as much as possible and where we have resorted to political jargon we have explained it directly or by context. The style is meant to be easy to read but that, however, does not mean that the content is simple! You might be well advised to come back to this book more than once. In places the style and approach might seem a little different, that is because different people have written different sections, but we have tried to make each author blend in smoothly with the next. If you just can't get on with the style of this book or make out what we are going on about then the fault is ours. We intend to bring out other versions of this book and use different mediums including audio and video.

THE EDITORS.

Introduction

● WHY CLASS WAR?

The Class War Federation is not another party seeking to gain power or a new way of telling you what to do. Class war is what happens when ordinary people have had enough of being pushed around and decide to fight back.

We live in a society severely split along the lines of class where capitalism, the State and the ruling class dominate. Our class, the working class, are here - at the centre of history. Indeed, all history to date is that of the conflict between us and our enemies who try to exploit and dominate us.

● A Sense of Tradition

The Class War Federation in Britain is part of a long and honourable tradition of working class resistance to oppression. We stand with the peasant revolts of 1381, 1450 and 1549, the Edinburgh 'Porteous' rising of 1736, the Levellers in the English civil war, the 'United Englishmen', the Luddites and 'General Lud', the East Anglia rising of 1816 and the 1820 Scottish Rising, the 'Captain Swing' rural workers revolts of 1830/31, the Bristol riots of 1831, the Pentridge and Grangemoor uprisings, the naval mutineers of the 18th, 19th and 20th centuries from Spithead to Invergordon, the army mutinies in India, the London Mob of the 19th century - the most political and feared mob in Europe that kept the Royal Family off the street! The 'Battle of the Braes' on the Isle of Skye, Scotland. The miners and railways strikes of 1910 and 1911, the heroic mutinies during and after World War One, the Glasgow and Luton rioters of 1919 (amongst many others), the general strikers of 1926, the unemployed workers movement battles with the police in the 1930's from Glasgow to Belfast to London, the 'Battle of Cable Street' in the East End of London against the police and fascists, the volunteers that went to fight fascism in Spain during the Spanish Civil War, the mutinies and strikes of World War Two, the soldiers squatting movement immediately after, the 'teabreak' strikers of the 1960's, the mass strikes of the 1970's and the battle of Saltley gate of 1972, the Grunwicks strikers of 1977, the 1979 Southall rising against the fascists and the police, the urban and rural rioters of the 1980's starting with Bristol in 1980, the great miners and printers strikes of the 1980's and the poll tax and prisoners revolt of 1990 when the jails and Central London burned! This is our tradition and our roots and we are proud of it.

We are still here. And until wage labour, capitalism and the State are destroyed there will always be a working class. The working class are a varied bunch of people who have certain things in common - as this book shows. The pathetic attempts to wish us out of existence by the middle class intellectuals of the Left and Right only confirm the crisis that their ruling class masters are experiencing in keeping control of us.

● The Failure of the Left

While there is much that is useful in the works of Marx, the interpretation that Lenin gave to him has been a complete disaster for our class here in Britain and around the world. Lenin's insistence on 'the Party' taking control of the revolution, the State and the capitalist economy was completely wrong.

During the early years of this century there was massive and growing conflict between our class and the capitalists all around the world. They were far more vulnerable then than they are now. Just before the First World War many felt we were on the edge of a Europe-wide revolution, but that war bought valuable time for the capitalists. Things came to a dramatic climax in Russia during the war in 1917. There, Lenin's Bolshevik party hi-jacked a popular revolt and ruthlessly destroyed opposition by the most advanced sections of the working class - the sailors of the Baltic fleet at Krondstat and the Ukrainian peasants movements amongst others. Lenin and Trotsky even prided themselves on the 'red terror' they had unleashed.

In our view the Russian revolution did not go wrong when Stalin seized power. It went wrong when the Bolsheviks seized control of the Soviets in October 1917, after the popular uprisings of February that year. The rise of the dictator Stalin was not an accident but a direct result of the policies of Lenin and the Bolsheviks. The same disastrous experience has been repeated all round the world where Lenin-inspired parties have seized power - in other words all the countries that have claimed to be 'communist', which is an insult to the meaning of the word. The tragedy of Russia has cost our class dear and set back the revolution many years, while the dead hand of Lenin has stifled development in the Left. Nowhere is this more true than of the British Left. It is only with the military, economic and political defeat of the Soviet capitalists by the Western capitalists that the Left are starting to reconsider what they have done - hardly inspiring confidence in their future performance.

There were people who saw the Bolsheviks and Lenin for what they were and suffered the organised wrath of the Communist Party such as John Maclean of Scotland. Later, the better members of the Party, such as Harry McShane, left after becoming aware that it was nothing more than a tool of Soviet foreign policy. Since then the British Communist Party has dissolved, changing its name and saying that class is no longer an issue.

From the tragedy of the USSR and Marxist-Leninism we move on to the farce of the British Left in the 1990's. This sorry collection does not make a pretty sight! The organised Left parties have all but collapsed in the face of the recent attacks of capitalism. This has been paralleled by a retreat of the 'intellectual' Left. Their main activity is now self-indulgent and obscure investigations into the meaning of capitalist culture. The end result of this long road of shame is the Left asserting that the working class either no longer exists or is of no importance. It's a strange coincidence that this is happening at the same time our society is becoming increasingly split along the lines of class and when attacks by the ruling class on us are becoming more and more savage, with resulting large increases in unemployment, homelessness and old-fashioned poverty.

We believe that one of the reasons for this failure of the Left lies in the fact that they are either composed of, or are controlled by, middle class people. A typical failing of the middle class (due to their conditioning) is to be unable to see beyond the end of their noses: they see the world as a reflection of themselves, and their hopes and concerns as the reality for others. To them the working class are merely stage props for their plans to "save the world" or reform capitalism. As a class they are encouraged to see themselves as 'the conscience of capitalism' - poor sods! Thus they approach left-wing groups with the same zeal and cruelty that their earlier generations took up missionary work in Africa.

The new concerns of the British Left now reflect the political, economic and cultural aspirations of the middle class more than ever before. Within the Left, and liberal movements such as ecology and feminism, debate is conducted within a narrow band of 'acceptable' options. This is hardly surprising. The privileged intellectual elites that compose these groups possess the means to make life uncomfortable for their ruling class masters but lack the will; their self-interest and laziness condone the misery and exploitation of others.

This explains why the choices the Left present to us are useless whether it is "Vote Labour Without Illusions" - by the Socialist Workers Party or support dictators like Saddam Hussein - by the Revolutionary Communist Party. Both are equally wrong and more importantly, equally harmless to capitalism.

Despite all this we acknowledge that there are many fine people doing good work in the Left and the anarchist movement who have a genuine commitment to the working class and revolution. We want to show them that there is another way and a better way.

● The Middle Class: An Important Warning

With all we have said so far you might think we hate all middle class people. Not so. Their class has a history of producing courageous

fighters against oppression that they can be well proud of. While there is much that is distasteful about the activities of the middle class as a whole we recognise the fact that before and during a revolution the middle class will split and part of it will side with our class. Just as we know that the working class will split during a revolution and part of it will side with the bosses.

Just promoting hatred for the middle classes obscures the real target of our anger - the ruling class. It is no coincidence that the fascists do exactly that, at the bidding of their ruling class masters. The middle class concern us as just another obstacle on the road to revolution, no more, no less.

We know only too well that revolution means civil war. If you are looking for Mickey Mouse politics you had better go elsewhere.

● The Class War Around the World

All over the world capitalism is running into huge problems and becoming increasingly unstable. The massive amount of debt in the world economy is like a time bomb ticking away. The three major trade blocs of North America, Europe and Japan are increasingly in competition with each other for markets and resources. They in turn are in conflict with the rest of the world for access to cheap resources and labour. The developing world is going to continue to get a hammering from the so-called First World nations both economically and militarily. Famine and desperate poverty are what many of our class are experiencing there. On top of this huge sums of money or to use the correct term - capital - are now moving around the world by electronic means in search of the quickest biggest profit. This is adding to the tendency of chaos in the capitalist system that many of us experience in our day to day lives.

The rise of the super trade blocs and 'loose' money means the nation-state is no longer as important for the capitalists as it once was - indeed it is now an obstruction. It is an obstruction because the capitalists want to move to ever larger forms of social and economic organisation. This rapid change around has left many of the European ruling classes behind, especially those involved in running the State such as senior politicians. Their solution is a wave of nationalism encouraged by these upper class groups who are scared of losing their sacred nation-state in the EEC. This is one of the reasons that ex-Prime Minister Maggie Thatcher got the boot from her mates. This wave of nationalism (Britain, France and Germany as well as that in Eastern Europe where it is leading headlong into bloody conflict) and its accompanying racism is also serving to distract us from the rapid re-organisation that the EEC is undergoing. It is going to be a super State with super-exploitation for our class, with the capitalists playing off one region against another for low wages. Whether this re-organisation of capitalism will go smoothly or disintergrate into chaos and war as in the USSR we cannot foretell.

● Imperialism is Alive and Well

Now, more than ever, the major capitalist powers and States, also called the "First World" or the "Developed World", need to intervene economically and militarily in other areas of the developing world where people and countries show any signs of breaking with or by-passing their control of the global economy. Some examples include; the United States in South America, Belgium and France in Africa, Britain in South Africa and the Falkland/Malvinas Islands. No area of the world can be allowed to go its own way. If it does it becomes a dangerous threat to the "world order" of capitalism. The stakes for the capitalists are huge. They desperately need to keep access to the markets and resources of the developing world.

"Between 25% and 33% of the exports of developed countries, and nearly 40% of US exports, go to the Third World. The major banks have lent many times their capital base to Third World countries and have made a fat profit in the process. Now the banks want their money back or at least to carry on making fat profits."

"AID - the West's False Handout" - Teresa Hayter, in *New Socialist* February 1985.

The so-called First World States are increasingly having to struggle to control and contain the economic changes in the developing world. This growing conflict is another source of instability and chaos in capitalism. To keep the upper hand in the world economy the First World will do nearly anything, and it is their actions here that give us the clearest picture of what we are up against. Famine, war, genocide, death squads and more, are what are people are facing around the world at the hands of the international ruling class and their regional supporters. Among the many examples that come to mind of this whole process are Ethiopia, Eritrea, Vietnam, Cambodia, East Timor, El

Salvador and Nicaragua.

Here, in countries like Britain, our biggest problem is ignorance, largely due to the media's distortions. Taking Vietnam and Nicaragua as examples the journalist John Pilger makes a good point;

"The United States gained a significant if partial victory [in Vietnam]. As Noam Chomsky has pointed out, American policy was never concerned with Vietnam alone, just as it was not concerned with Nicaragua alone. In Vietnam the short term "threat" came from a nationalist leadership concerned with domestic needs rather than with the demands of the United States. The long-term threat to America was that of a development model which other countries might have followed; and exactly the same was true of the Nicaraguan "threat". Far from being beaten in South East Asia, the United States has devastated, blockaded and isolated Vietnam and its "virus" and has subordinated to American interests almost every regime in the region."

"Heroes" - John Pilger.

When we say the choice facing us is barbarism or revolution we are quite serious.

● Ireland

Nationalism is one of the key ways of keeping our class divided. At the moment Britain is fighting an extremely dirty colonial war in Ireland that any banana republic could be proud of. That this war has gone on so long is a measure of the strength and arrogance of British nationalism. The scale and courage of the resistance to the British State in Ireland is massive. The response of much of the Left and anarchists is shameful. On one hand there is the cynical opportunism of groups like the Revolutionary Communist Party (RCP), while on the other hand groups like Militant and some of the anarchists just splutter a load of reactionary, moralistic nonsense at every outbreak of violence. Ireland is a classic case of the false choices that the Left present our class with. One is that the IRA, INLA etc. should have our unconditional support, the other is that they are just evil murdering scum! We are not impressed with this. The IRA, Sinn Fein, INLA etc. do not have unconditional support in Ireland from their own supporters - there is criticism, naturally. As for viewing the Republicans as evil, murdering scum, we suppose those groups that take this view would say the same of anybody who uses violence against oppression.

To those that say the struggle in Ireland is merely a nationalist one we say no. Of course nationalism is present (as it is in every struggle against the occupying forces of imperialism) but it is not the only element involved. We have much to learn from the Irish struggle against the British State and from similar struggles elsewhere. *Please see Chapter One and the Irish appendix for further discussion.*

● MOVEMENTS ORGANISATIONS AND REVOLUTIONARIES

These things mean many different things to many people. Its best to be clear about what we mean right at the start.

● Movements

When we say create a "working class movement" we are not talking about the Class War Federation or any other political group. The "movement" we have in mind is a large and growing number of people that come from very different backgrounds, experiences and places to work together to destroy capitalism and the State. This movement will be very diverse in nature yet it will have clear agreement on basic ideas. Within this movement there will be a variety of organisations reflecting different backgrounds and needs. The control of this movement will not lie in any party, central committee or group of intellectuals, power will lie in the hands of people themselves. Such a movement is far from being a pipe dream. It is the engine that drives the revolution, history is full of examples (Russia, Spain, Nicaragua, Cuba, Portugal.)

● Organisations

Political organisations exist to achieve certain objectives. One of the objectives of the Class War Federation is to help in the creation of an international working class movement as outlined above. As far as we are concerned the more organisations that exist to further these kind of basic objectives the better.

● Revolutionaries

There is no such thing as a full-time 'professional' revolutionary, although there are people who think they are! We are 'amateurs' and combine revolutionary work with everyday life. In the process we change and so do our lives. Revolutionaries are ordinary people who do extraordinary things.

● The Class War Federation

The Federation contains people who may describe themselves as anarchist, communists or socialist. More important than these 'off the shelf labels' is what these people really think and what brings them together. We believe that the ideas and politics you have are more important than what you call them. There are no pure traditions. Anarchism was a split from the communist movement as a reaction to authoritarian Marxism. It is important that we should learn from the past to make the 'politics of today'. We feel that the Left, including the anarchists, have forgotten some of the basics that earlier generations of revolutionaries and class warriors knew so well. We don't intend to allow ourselves to forget the two most basic tools that a good revolutionary needs; firstly, is to be able to communicate clearly with other working class people in every possible way. As an older revolutionary pointed out when looking at the Left in the 1970's;

"The intellectuals are writing for one another instead of for working class people; they seem to think that workers can't read!"
Harry McShane.

Secondly is the need to care about people - and each other. And, just to set the record straight: the Class War Federation does not think that music, drugs or fashion will change the world. The Federation has no links with, or interest in, the animal rights movement.

Throughout this book there are quotations from past and present writers. These are intended to help illustrate our ideas and show some of the sources and traditions we draw on as inspiration. They do not indicate complete agreement with that authors ideas.

We hope that after reading this book you will be stirred to participate in the fight against oppression and that questions will be raised that you will have to find answers to. Of course we would like you to get involved with the Class War Federation but more than that we hope that you and others get together to fight back in your own ways.

OUR TIME HAS COME.

Chapter 1

Capitalism

"The great only appear great because we are on our knees. Let us rise."
James Connolly-*Edinburgh born Irish socialist.*

Section Headings
- Introduction.
- Capitalism - What it is.
- Understanding Capitalism.
- Capitalism in the 20th Century.
- A Summary of Capitalism.
- Prospects for Change.

• INTRODUCTION

Our daily lives are completely dominated by two distinct but closely related forces that control all aspects of our society. They are capitalism and the State. Here we are going to deal with capitalism. The State will be covered in Chapter Two.

• CAPITALISM - WHAT IT IS

This is the name given to the way the economic or productive forces of society are organised at the moment. As it's name implies the main activity involved is the creation and accumulation of capital - represented by money and property. It is this activity that determines the way our present society works and is at the foundation of our present way of life.

Capitalism did not appear overnight. Before it there was another sort of society called feudalism where the economic organisation was on a different footing. There the ruling class simply took what they wanted by force, in the form of tributes of produce and crops etc. from the peasants and tithes to the church. This whole society was justified and supported by the church who in return got their 10%. This sort of economy was based on the ownership of land and represented a preindustrial method of production.

From this older form of society grew modern capitalism through a mixed process of economic changes and reforms. In Britain where capitalism started first, this has been a lengthy process. In other countries capitalism has been installed in a far shorter time-span. Nevertheless, wherever you live in the world you live in a capitalist society: - the USA, UK, USSR, Cuba, S.Africa, India etc. are all capitalist economies. The actual practice varies from place to place but the essentials of capitalist society are now universal in this world. The State now fills many of the functions (e.g. welfare) that the church played under feudalism - more on this in Chapter Two. It is time we described the bare essentials of capitalism.

● How Capitalism Works

To exist capitalism has to have society organised in a certain way, often called the social relations of capitalism. Here we list them;

● Everything, and we mean everything, must have a price to enable it to be sold for money.

● To get hold of the things needed for life - food, housing, clothes, entertainment etc. money is needed. For most people the only way to get money is by selling their labour in return for a wage. These people are generally called the working class. They have little or no productive property i.e. property that is employed in creating profit. Interest on savings or a rise in the value of your house are not profit. Interest is the rent you are paid by the capitalist for the use of your money. House price increases and decreases are a side effect on the economy of the activities of the capitalists and represent the periodic re-valuing of resources by the capitalists.

● The goods and services that people produce by their labours (mental and physical) are sold by their employers for a profit. This profit comes from two causes:-

● Labour; the labour used in making the product.

● The market; being able to sell the product for a price that will ensure a profit.

● This profit is stored as capital in the form of money and property.

● As the things that are produced are sold for a profit it follows that the wage earners only receive a part of the value or wealth that their labour produces. The people who take the profit are the capitalists. This is the trick! The capital in capitalism comes from the labour of the working class. Someone explained this well at the start of this century and called it "The Great Money Trick", *(See below for an explanation)*.

● Not content with exploiting us at work the capitalists take a second hit at us by selling us back the product of our labours. As consumers we have to pay directly or indirectly for everything we need to live.

● In capitalism there are many divisions fostered in the workforce to keep wages down and the working class divided. Racism and sexism are the most profitable divisions from the capitalist's point of view (more on this later).

● Capitalists compete with each other to make profit.

● The working classes have to compete against each other to survive in the market for labour. This has the effect of tending to put us in a defensive position.

● The prime, and most fundamental, reasons for the existence of capitalism and the capitalist are;

  ● To continue making a profit in order to accumulate more capital.

  ● To increase the amount and rate of profit if at all possible.

● War is good for capitalism because lots of products and services are destroyed and have to be replaced over and over again, meaning lots of profit at every stage of the produce and consume cycle.

These are the driving forces behind capitalism and its only explanation. This is the grim reality of capitalism as a way of organising society. The satisfaction of human needs and desires are not important, except in the interests of profit and stability.

● The Great Money Trick!

"How is it that the benefits of civilisation are not produced for the benefit of all? How is it that the majority of the people always have to go without most of the refinements, comforts, and pleasures of life, and very often without even the bare necessaries of existence? Plenty of materials, plenty of labour, plenty of machinery - and nearly everybody going short of nearly everything!

The present money system prevents us from doing the necessary work, and consequently causes the majority of the population to go short of the things that can be made by work. They suffer want in the means of producing abundance. They remain idle because they are bound and fettered with a chain of gold."

From "The Ragged Trousered Philanthropists" by Robert Tressel.

See the Appendix for his full explanation of "The Great Money Trick" where he describes how wage-labour is at the heart of capitalism. He briefly mentions how capitalism is always getting into trouble and introduces the idea of the problem of over production in capitalism, which we pick up on at the end of this chapter.

● UNDERSTANDING CAPITALISM

As human beings we all have certain needs and desires that have to be satisfied if we are to continue living and enjoy life; good housing, food and drink, healthcare, education, leisure facilities and so on.

In a capitalist society only some of these needs and desires are fulfilled and then only for profit and stability. But because we are told that capitalism is 'natural', inevitable and has no alternative, we look to it to provide us with what we need, and most of us are doomed to disappointment. Ideas like; "a fair days work for a fair days pay", "value for money", "fair competition", "buy British", "keep foreigners out" "respect for the law", are accepted by many people and are used to justify our present situation, when of course they do not exist for the capitalist!

The vast majority of people in the UK and the rest of the world do not have enough of even the basics to lead a happy life; decent housing, good food, leisure, worth while work etc.

What we do have lots of are boredom, frustration, unemployment, poverty, poor housing, poor food or none at all, poor health, severe social divisions along the lines of race, sex, age, sexuality (meaning whether you prefer the opposite sex or not), a popular culture that is imposed from above, whether it is respect for the rich and love of Royalty as in the UK. Or belief in the Party in the so-called communist countries or fear of a religious or military dictator. This is the reality of capitalism for most people.

To stabilise such a miserable society we are encouraged to believe that we are responsible as individuals for our own position in society or that our position is a result of divine forces.

● In the Beginning - (a mini history of capitalism)

The start of the economic end of feudalism was matched by the emergence of the Protestant religion to replace the Roman Catholic one. This new religion was much more suited to the earthly interests of the merchants and craftmasters who were the forerunners of the capitalists. They also required an economy where everything could be exchanged for money. The growing need for gold and silver to act as currency was what drove the Spanish and others to the Americas and was one of the earliest examples of capitalist imperialism, much more was to follow.

At first this capitalist class just did what they did previously on a larger scale. But they had political ambitions to have a different society with different values so they got rid of the weak feudal kings and aristocracy, as in the French revolution, or came to terms with them and incorporated them into a new ruling class as in Britain. Here the aristocracy remained in control of the civil service and influenced the development of the British State machine and ruling class right up to the present;

"It is as well to recall the continuing enormous power of the landed aristocracy (however much their wealth comes now from other sources). No cabinet between 1830 and 1900 had less than 41% of an aristocratic element."

"The Great Arch" - by Corrigan and Sayer.

This ability to integrate new cliques into the ruling class is one of the strengths of the British ruling class. The 'link' that cements the old and new rulers is the possession of profitable property. This new ruling class came to be called the "bourgeoisie". Having obtained political power through control of the State (more later) they then started a thorough re-organisation of society in line with their own interests and values. *See the appendix on The History of Capitalism for a fuller history.*

● Capitalism and the World (the international division of labour)

● Imperialism

This, as we pointed out above, has been central to capitalism right from the start and has accounted for its expansion. By this we mean the theft of resources and labour from people in other parts of the world by force. Some classic examples:

● Slavery - the kidnapping of Africans, and others, for use as slaves in the Caribbean and American cotton and sugar plantations.

● The stealing of tea, coffee, cocoa, gold, rubber, wood, food, cotton, minerals etc. from the people forced into the British, French, German, Dutch, Spanish, and Belgian Empires - to mention but a few.

● It is also the forcing of other people to be a market for your products and so making them dependant on your economy, like cotton clothes to India and Opium to China.

This is what made Britain 'Great'. This imperialism has left a deep scar on our class in the form of the racism that justifies its outrages. In countries like Britain, France, the USA and Germany it still cripples our unity.

Writing of the Black slave rebellions in the French colony of Haiti in the late 18th century C.L.R. James notes how imperialism and its cruelties are a constant feature of the history of capitalism

"The French burned alive, hanged, drowned, tortured, and started again their old habit of burying blacks up to their neck near nests of insects. It was not only hatred and fear but policy.... It was the policy of the Tories that the British followed in Ireland in 1921 [and today] regardless of the complaints of the Guardian newspaper or the pacifists. So it is, so it has always been."

From "The Black Jacobins" - by C.L.R. James.

● Colonialism

This is a development of imperialism. Having taken a land and its people into servitude, the imperial power often sent settlers to it to form a local ruling class and recruit a group of native supporters. These native supporters often carry on the work of the settlers after the colonial power has withdrawn e.g. the Lebanon, India and South Africa. Armed force, religion and cultural manipulation in the form of denial of language and identity are typical of this process. Once in place colonialism is a more efficient way of running a colony than sheer force. Examples include: Hong Kong, Northern Ireland, North America under the British, Lebanon under the French, and the Philippines under the USA.

● The Sexual and Racial Division of Labour

Capitalism does not just create an international division of labour as in imperialism and colonialism but an internal social division of labour. We are referring here to the sexual and racial divisions of labour. We have to be clear in our minds that racism and sexism occur not just because people are bigots; they are a direct result of capitalism's need to divide up the workforce on a permanent basis. The racial and sexual division of labour fragments sections of the workforce from each other and justify the super-exploitation of workers in weaker economic positions like women, ethnic and immigrant workers.

● The Sexual Division of Labour

Even though the discrimination against women predates capitalism (and was largely created by religion), the economic exploitation of women has become an integral part of our economic system. Here we look at the difference between women's work and men's work. Although many women in the UK are employed, it is nearly always in low paid and part-time jobs. But even more far reaching than this is the huge amount of work that women do which is unpaid, such as housework, cooking, child care etc. This unpaid work services the domestic needs of the existing generation of workers (men and women) for free, and rears the next generation of workers for the capitalist entirely free of charge. You do not have to be a genius to see why this is a good deal for the capitalist class. This situation is the

economic foundation of discrimination against women called sexism, which as a class we must overcome to move forwards. *Please refer to Chapter Three for further discussion of sexism.*

Needless to say the capitalist will never pay more than a pittance for this work. The idea of "wages for housework" is an illusion. We believe the only real solution to low pay and no pay for women is the removal of capitalism.

With women's work tending to be less permanent and low paid their position in the economy is similar to the unemployed. Together they form a section of the workforce which has a below average status in the job-market and are a source of cheap labour. Bosses can use and discard them at will when they are no longer required. This part of the workforce were called "The Reserve Army of Labour" by Marx for fairly obvious reasons. The existence and use of this reserve army by the capitalists has the general effect of reducing the wages of the entire working class and sapping our militancy and unity. Workers from this reserve can be brought in to replace others who have been sacked. For those of us living in this sub-section of the workforce it can mean a life of permanent poverty with little hope of getting out of that situation. On the area of women's work and unemployment the unions have done little or no organising in the past, and show little or no enthusiasm for doing any in the future.

● The Racial Division of Labour

Ethnic groups (whether immigrant or permanently resident) that are different from the majority in the UK are another sub-section of the workforce and are often a part of the reserve army of labour mentioned above.

The racial division of labour came into full effect after World War Two, with the increase of immigration from Commonwealth countries to fill the shortage of labour in the UK economy during the boom years. Despite fighting on the same side in the war and having skills, they were shunted off into low paid, semi-skilled or unskilled work, and poor housing. They were destined to become a separate part of the working class. This was the economic basis of racism. The traditional racism of the British ruling class justified this treatment of these people to the rest of the white working class. *See Chapter Three for more on racism.*

Asian workers were mostly concentrated in the textile industries and foundries. The Afro-Caribbeans were mostly concentrated in the low paid service sector jobs like cleaning, building, buses and nursing - where white immigrant groups like the Irish were also concentrated. In the workplace ethnic groups were concentrated in particular sectors of production (usually the lowest paid, menial, unsocial hours, dirty and dangerous work). It was not unusual for there to be 'ethnic shifts' in factories which isolated black workers even more from white workers (please note that when we say 'black' we mean all non white people).

The response of the trade unions to this situation has been, as with women and the unemployed, another chapter of shame. The official union bureaucracy has sabotaged and ignored militant actions taken by black workers to improve their work conditions or pay and to stop discrimination. Black workers have had to rely on their own communities and their own working class organisations for help. The black experience at work, as well as that of women, fits in with the general working class's experience of the unions leadership: sabotaging anything that rocks the boat and threatens real radical changes. This behaviour we call "collaboration with the enemy" and intend to treat it accordingly. The racial division of labour and the racism that justifies it, is crucial to capitalist economic domination. It presents another barrier to a united working class, as does sexism, and if we wish to achieve anything we have to attack and destroy both.

● CAPITALISM IN THE 20th CENTURY

Towards the end of the 19th century, ownership of enterprises started to move away from individuals to that of groups of shareholders. Here the role of "management" became more important, although many also were large shareholders. This process intensified as companies grew larger as they gobbled each other up to form monopolies that dominated the market for certain products in certain areas of the world. At this stage capitalists were tied closely to the interests of their own nation-states e.g. oil, coal, shipping, manufacturing, railways, banks etc. In most cases the two coincided. Where they did not, there was usually a civil war to enable the dominant group of capitalists to take over. The American civil war is a good example of this. It was a war between two groups of capitalists and not about slavery as the recent rewriting of history would have us believe. Competition between capitalists was, and is, fierce for markets and resources. This was often resolved by the means of war between different nation-states representing different capitalists.

The First World War was the culmination of this competition among the international capitalists. After the war capitalism continued to expand all over the world through imperialism and the pickings were rich. Britain had just about all of the Middle East, most of the Far East and Africa. This period saw the emergence of companies that had operations all around the world.

The trend to shareholder owned capitalism continued with an increase in the numbers of the very rich as shareholders, and the growing trend for companies and financial institutions to hold shares in other companies. The great international economic crisis of the 1920's and 30's marked a turning point in capitalist economics. Up till then there had been a succession of re-workings of Adam Smiths' (the capitalist economist) ideas, mostly all concerned to balance freedom for the capitalist with social stability. At the time of the great depression in the USA, the work of the economist Dr. Simon N. Patten held sway in government circles. He argued for the minimum of government intervention rather like the present fashion in the USA and the UK. Thus the response of the government was to step aside in the belief that the economy would sort itself out. This experiment in business self-management proved disastrous. It resulted in the restriction of production, the squeezing out of small businesses and the tendency to trample down everyone in the pursuit of profit - so deepening the effect of the depression.

A new group of economists, of whom John Maynard Keynes is the best known, learnt their lesson from the great depression and realised that capitalism could not be left to its own devices. They started to take a long term view of things and increased the trend towards bureaucracy, with the role of management growing further and the increasing participation of State bodies in large scale economic management and planning. They saw the State as having the function of an economic regulator. The logical progression was to world-wide bodies to regulate capitalism, hence the development of the World Bank and the International Monetary Fund (IMF) who are so powerful today.

● Trade Unions

By the beginning of the 20th century capitalism had drastically changed from the beginning of the 19th century. Large industrial centres such as those in Northern Ireland, the West of Scotland and South Wales were employing huge numbers of workers in coal, iron and steel, engineering, and textiles etc. Advances in production led to the removal of many skilled workers from industry, the workforce came to be made up of large numbers of labourers, machine minders and semi-skilled workers. Capitalism was entering the era of mass production and a crisis of its own making, that of producing more than it could sell on the existing market. This a recurring crisis in capitalism.

These huge numbers of working class people all living in great cities working close to each other, sharing similar conditions and experiences at work and at home, not surprisingly started to share common problems and hopes. The workplace became the centre of renewed attempts to improve the conditions of life by demands for higher wages and shorter hours. Faced with a decline in profits and an increasingly militant workforce the capitalists became very vulnerable to attack at the workplace. Just before the First World War there were many large and bitter strikes in Britain. Many believed we were on the brink of revolution, as this report on the period from "*Merseyside Anarchist*" very graphically shows;

"*The years before World War One saw an explosion of class warfare in Britain not seen since the Chartist movement of the early*

19th century. Known as the "Labour Unrest" or "Syndicalist Revolt", this period saw the rapid escalation of strike action - insurgent in character, largely unofficial, and often violent. Trade union membership doubled from around 2,500,000 in 1909, to over 4,000,000 by 1914 - while days lost due to industrial action rose from around 2,500,000 a year in 1909 to nearly 41,000,000 a year in 1912.

The first major unrest centred on the South Wales coalfields. In the Cambrian Combine strike of September 1910 to August 1911, striking miners formed mass pickets, intercepted trains, and attacked scabs, working pits, and managers' houses. At Tonypandy one striker was killed by the police. In 1911 the strike wave spread to the transport industry. Between June and August 1911 strikes took place in all the major ports - starting with seaman and soon extending to dockers and other groups of workers in factories and processing plants. In August an unofficial walkout by railwaymen on Merseyside escalated into the first national railway strike and a General Transport Strike on Merseyside. On Merseyside two strikers were shot dead by troops during street fighting - as crowds attacked prison vans taking prisoners to Walton jail. In Llanelly (S.Wales) two workers were also shot dead, and crowds bayonet charged - strikers in turn tore up rail tracks, damaged signal boxes and telegraph systems, and set fire to trucks. In 1912 another transport strike broke out in London, and the miners came out again - this time nationally.

1913 saw the strike wave spreading to many groups of workers previously unaffected - semi-skilled and unskilled engineering workers in the West Midlands "Black Country Strike", the Leeds Corporation Strike etc. the Dublin Lockout of August 1913 to January 1914, against the Irish Transport Workers Union, led to five deaths, and over 650 jailed, and the formation of the Irish Citizens Army as a workers defence force. Back in Britain, rising unoffical strikes in the building industry in 1913 came to a head with a bitter five month lockout in 1914. Many smaller strikes also took place during this period. Meanwhile, the formation of the National Transport Workers Federation in 1910, the National Union of Railwaymen in 1912 and the Triple Alliance - a solidarity pact between miners, transport workers and railwaymen - in 1914, seemed to lay the groundwork for more effective solidarity between unions.

Increasingly, as conflict continued and attitudes hardened with the onset of a new economic downturn, Britain seemed to be rushing headlong towards mass industrial revolt, if not an insurgent General

Strike. As the atmosphere of crisis intensified, it took the outbreak of war in August 1914 to bring the movement to a halt."

"The Syndicalist Revolt" - taken from *"Merseyside Anarchist".*

The war was one part of the solution for the capitalists to this problem, it used up a lot of capital (and people), diverted working class anger into patriotism, destroyed competing capitalists in Germany and opened up new markets abroad. The second part of the solution was the legalising of trade unions to represent the working class. With, of course, the moderate and reformist leaders within the unions being encouraged by the capitalists, and the revolutionary workers being penalised.

Just after the First World War capitalism was again in trouble internationally and in Britain, there was massive social and industrial unrest. The divided and reformist trade unions just held the line for capitalism, despite the heroic efforts of many workers and activists. By the time of the General Strike in 1926, the absorption of the unions within the capitalist machine was complete, the leadership had sold out.

As a member of the ruling class put it looking back at this period;

"Trade union organisation was the only thing between us and anarchy".

Lord Balfour.

The reformist and paternal trade unions in the workplace were paralleled by the formation of the Labour Party in the community. The ruling class had very clear ideas on the benefits of this. Lloyd George and Stanley Baldwin made it clear that they wanted the Labour Party incorporated within the State machine of parliamentary politics. Their view was that this would add to the stability of the State by bringing in the moderate elements and leave the radicals on the 'outside'. In this way trade unions and the Labour Party became essential for the smooth running of capitalism from 1920 until 1975, a role which they happily played.

But later the situation changed completely and from 1975 onwards the unions and the Labour Party came under increasing attack in Britain.

In the 1980's the powers of the unions were severely limited as capitalism moved into a new phase, where the co-operation of the labour movement was no longer required. Now in the new conditions of capitalism, and its present economic crisis, the ruling class have gone back to their 19th century methods where negotiation and co-operation have no place in their plans. They are in such trouble that they know they are going to have to impose new conditions on the working class both at work and in the community.

This need of the ruling class has found its political expression in a philosophy called "The New Right" in the USA and the UK. In essence, this a return to the ideas of the 19th century with the emphasis being on the survival of the fittest, and enterprise. When the British ex-Prime Minister, Margaret Thatcher, said she did not believe in 'society', she meant this; that society was going to be transformed into a battle for survival bringing a new age of barbarism.

The response of the trade unions and labour movement to this attack has been to collapse and take up the new rights' ideas, calling this 'the new realism'. This collapse by the leadership of the labour movement has happened despite the bitter struggles of workers at the shop floor level. Not surprisingly we do not look to the unions to deliver a better way of life for our class. Capitalism must, and will be fought in the workplace (at the point of production as it's sometimes called), but the unions will not be the tool.

● After World War Two

The Second World War was again a competition between capitalists; the fascist 'Axis' and the 'Allies'. For both it was also a solution to the economic crisis of the depression guaranteeing a high return of profit. The English socialist William Morris made the perceptive observation that,

"War is the natural and healthy state of capitalism. Both war between individuals and war between countries,"

For the USA, World War Two saved the day. In 1940 before they entered the war, military spending stood at 3.2% of the Gross National Product (GNP), note that the GNP is simply the value of everything including services produced by a country. In 1943 it stood at 40% of the GNP, with profits reaching unprecedented heights. Military production still dominates the USA economy because of the 'Cold War' with the Soviet Union. In 1988 the Pentagon awarded $142 billion in defence contracts. This economy is based on war, as we pointed out earlier, war is good for capitalism as it consumes lots of money (capital) and returns high profit. This is one of the reasons that the Gulf War, and before it, Vietnam started.

After World War Two the world was carved up again between the victors. Fascism and capitalism are two sides of the same coin. There were many people who felt that it was a fight against fascism and fought with great courage and sacrifice, which should not be sneered at by us. Many of our families still bear the scars. However the war was a conflict between capitalists and not a war to end capitalism itself.

The spread of international capitalism leapt forward again with the aid of imperialism - that of the USA and USSR particularly. The 1950's and 60's saw the expansion of ever larger firms around the world like Exxon, BP, ITT, Glaxo, Ford, Proctor and Gamble etc. These large international companies came to be called multi-national on account of the fact that they operated across different countries on a global scale. They came to have their own economic and political ambitions and were able to exert enormous pressure on individual countries. The emerging independence movements in Asia and Africa had to come to terms with these multinationals who controlled the markets for their domestic produce and resources.

Although these multinationals have their own ambitions, they do identify with certain nation-states to benefit from the political and military support they can give. Still, the idea of a patriotic capitalist is a joke. During the Falklands/Malvinas war Lloyds Bank, which had a large interest in Argentina, traded there as normal. During the First World War the khaki dye for British Army uniforms was bought from Germany and during the bitter Iran/Iraq war in the 1980's both sides continued dealing and swopping oil credits on the international market.

● Consumerism and Imperialism - After World War Two

After World War Two the capitalist victors on the allied side faced a set of problems; What were they to do with the huge amount of capital accumulated from the profits of five years of a world-wide war? And how were they going to manage the enormous productive capabilities and technology that they now owned?

Their solution was dictated by the capitalist principles of self-preservation and increased profit. In practice this resulted in consumerism in the industrialised world and imperialism in the Third World. This, together with the application of Keynes's economics, bought more time for capitalism - about another twenty five years until the end of the 1960's.

● Consumerism

This was the method they found to use the means of production and technology that they controlled. Essentially it was the production of more of everything, and more and more exotic and luxury products. Where no market existed for goods they were created through the increasingly powerful and sophisticated media industry of TV, radio and newspapers. We became the market for this consumerism, and in turn the workforce to produce the products, which sums up nicely the essential cycle of capitalism. The work of economist Thornstein Veblen concentrated on this. He saw consumerism as a way of creating an endless system of social ranking and snobbery which reflected the ruling class's obsession with social standing and privilege. Veblen saw this as an effective way of tying the workforce to the economic system, where everything we own represents our standing in society and the pressure is constantly on us to buy new objects to 'move up'.

A classic example of this process was the massive growth in car ownership that continues to this day. This was pushed very strongly by the interested parties; car producers, steel firms, engineering firms, civil engineers, roadhauliers etc. A perfectly good national rail system was destroyed by government decree to force us onto the roads. All that remained was to market the ideas to us, and if you find this hard to grasp just look how much time and money is spent selling cars to us today. This is a classic example of the illusion of the idea of "the Free Market". There is of course no free market, nor will there ever be. What the phrase means is that they are free to exploit us.

Now we are at the advanced stage of consumerism and can look back over forty-five years of what amounts to chaos in human terms. We have traffic jams over one hundred miles long on the motorways, and many of us can walk to work faster than we could drive there! We have thousands of products that we are 'free' to choose from, provided we have the money to pay for them. Meanwhile our basic human needs of good housing, healthcare, food, education, leisure and worthwhile work have not been met.

In the early 1970's some French writers expressed the situation as follows,

"Wage labour itself has been an absurdity for several decades. It forces one part of the workers to engage in exhausting factory work;

another part which is very numerous in countries like the USA and the UK, work in the unproductive sector i.e. insurance, banking, advertising, sales etc. The function of this sector is to make sales easier, and to absorb workers rejected by mechanisation and automation, thus providing a mass of consumers, and being another aspect of crisis management. Capital takes possesion of all the sciences and technologies: in the productive field, it orients research towards study of what will bring a maximum profit; in the unproductive field, it develops management and marketing"

From "The Eclipse and Re-emergence of the Communist Movement" - by Barrot and Martin.

● Post War Imperialism

The massive post war economic boom that was built on consumerism in the industrial world of the USA, Japan, Europe etc., was also founded on the continuing direct and brutal exploitation of people and resources in the Third World. Their labour and land is used to produce cheap raw materials for the industrial countries; coffee, tea, cocoa, bauxite, copper, iron, uranium, rice, rubber, wood, cotton and so on. The prices of these raw materials have remained stagnant or dropped in the last ten or twenty years, like tin in the Far East and cocoa in Africa. These areas are also a target for fairly useless exports from the First World; hi-tech armaments, nuclear power, consumer goods e.g. coca-cola and cigarettes.

While people in the First World suffer boredom, depression, unemployment, poor housing and inadequate health care the people of the Third World have all that plus famine and war.

● The Present (1960-1990)

At present capitalism has achieved a truly global economy dominated by multinationals and some strong nation-states. All these are controlled by a mixture of rich individuals, financial institutions - and a very highly placed powerful managerial class that governs the large corporations and international co-ordinators of capitalism like the World Bank, IMF and some lesser known groups (Tri-Lateral Commission etc.)

There are factions in this class, who often clash with each other with dire results for our class around the world. (E.g. Saddam Hussein and the Kuwaiti ruling class). But remember, they are united when it comes to doing business and attacking us.

● A SUMMARY OF CAPITALISM

So what conclusions can we come to about capitalism?

● It is an economic system run purely for profit and in the interests of a small class, the capitalists, and at the expense of the largest class, the working class. The whole of present society is dominated by the needs of capitalism.

● Our human needs cannot be met by capitalism.

● Relationships between people are dominated by the ideas and values behind capitalism.

● Capitalism is not a machine governed by natural laws as Marx tended to suggest. It is a simple economic system run by a group of people who compete fiercely with each other, learn from their mistakes (sometimes) and try to plan ahead. The people who we call capitalists are only partly in control of the worldwide capitalist economy. The rest of the time it follows its own cycle of produce, consume, profit, invest, - produce, consume, profit, invest etc. Capitalism is part machine, part wild beast with the ruling class sometimes controlling it. It is chaos.

● It is not inevitable that capitalism will die of its own accord. Therefore it should be destroyed and replaced by a way of life that takes as its first principle;

"From each according to their ability and to each according to their need"

From "The Communist Manifesto" - Karl Marx.

So that what is produced is not determined by the values of profit and greed, as at the moment. Between these two opposing views of how the productive forces of society should be organised there can be no peace. It is war. For us the prize is a world that will be fit for us and our children to live in, where the abilities, needs and desires of people are fully realised. This way of life has been called anarchism, communism and socialism; the crucial thing is to end capitalism and the social relations that go with it that make our lives miserable.

● Capitalism is not based on taking account of human needs or the limits of the natural world. It runs according to its own set of simple rules. At times it enters severe crisis of its own making, such as the crisis of over-production, fall of profit, surplus of capital, failure of natural resources and, of course, resistance from us. Capitalism is a 'young' economic system compared to what went before. Karl Marx tried to show that it was fundamentally unstable according to its own rules, and was substantially correct. Various Left parties have predicted that this or that crisis is the final crisis and have been left with egg on their faces. Capital's managers, the ruling class, try to avoid crisis and try to plan ahead with varying degrees of success. Either way we do not intend to wait around for capitalism to self-destruct. *(See Appendix on Karl Marx).*

● Capitalism has no hard and fast creed, dogma, or hereditary leadership. Unlike peculiar religious customs, it can adapt. In essence it reduces all individuals to financial relations with each other. That is to say whether you believe in Christ or Allah, support the Royal Family or Nelson Mandela, the bottom line is; it's how much money you've got in your pocket that allows you to live by buying the next meal, a place to live, or latest consumer goods etc. Everything; sex, rebellion, health, freedom, leisure, all are given price tags. Everything is bought and sold.

So there you have it. Capitalism, it is a system that has done nothing, and continues to do nothing for us except to create the right

conditions and instruments to bring about a social revolution. So what are we waiting for?

● PROSPECTS FOR CHANGE

As we pointed out earlier capitalism is not a stable economic system and regularly suffers crises, which we, the working class, have to invariably pay for in one form or another. Below we briefly describe the problems that capitalism has created for itself, and end by describing how and why, as an economic system it is regularly going to enter crisis of its own creation. We conclude that it is not inevitable that it will die of its own accord and that we must destroy it.

● The Problems Facing Capitalism

Profit; in the late 20th century we are faced with a group of very large international companies competing for limited markets. This raises the problem of profitability. The mad thing about capital is that it is totally useless unless it is used or re-employed in making more profit that becomes more capital. But the more capital that is generated, the more the capitalist must try to re-employ it and so on. Eventually the capitalist starts to run out of things to make a profit from and then enters into a crisis, called the 'crisis of over production' by Marx. This is one of the fundamental problems within capitalism and is what makes it so unstable. A fuller description of this is given at the end of this chapter.

Enviroment; a truly world economy that has caused environmental destruction on such a global scale that the managers of capitalism are having to work it into their plans for the future (would you believe that this includes working out the replacement value of the Amazonian rainforest! Its true, the IMF and World Bank have done so).

Restructuring; since the late 1960's capitalism has been undergoing a big re-organisation of its international structure, hence the name. This has many caused problems. Here is a brief description of re-structuring and its main effect. The continuing transfer of basic manufacturing industry from the First World to so-called Second World countries occurs because the drastically lower wages there mean more profit. Some examples include; shoe manufacture to Brazil and Egypt, steel products to China, shipbuilding to Korea, textiles to Singapore and chemicals to India (remember Bhopal?). Coping with the resulting unemployment in the First World is a problem.

The emergence of certain areas in the world, where the control and management of capital on an international scale are becoming one of the central economic activities of the countries concerned. Examples include; the Hitachi corporation in Japan which is an international company in its own right, producing electronic consumer goods and heavy engineering plant, yet makes more profit out of its investment activities than its manufacturing. The same is true of the BMW company of Germany.

This trend is accompanied by a growing computer and information industry that is needed to service the finance sector. A booming service sector also goes with this growth of the wealthy, and not so wealthy, finance workers from yuppies to bank clerks. These countries are becoming effectively the 'management centres' of global capitalism. Their societies are grossly distorted as a result of the enormous growth in this sector and the transfer of manufacturing industry to the Second and Third World. As a result countries like the UK are now very dependant on international finance. The dramatic decline of service industry employment in the South East of England during the recession of the early 1990's is an example of this dependence. Meanwhile the Third World suffers as a result of the resources diverted away from it.

Our French friends have described this growth of "capital management" and its effects;

"The problems caused by buying and selling, by the realisation of the value of the product on the market, create a complex mechanism, including credit, banking, insurance and advertising. Capital becomes a sort of parasite absorbing a huge and growing part of society's total resources in the costs of the 'management' of value. Bookeeping, which is a necessary function in any developed social organisation, has now become a ruinous and bureaucratic machine overwhelming society and real needs instead of helping to fulfil them"

From "The Eclipse and Re-emergence of the Communist Movement." - Barrot and Martin.

This, together with severe unemployment due to removal of manufacturing industry is creating a severely divided society compared to the 1945-1970 period in the UK. The prospect of intense, internal unrest is a very real, and for our bosses a very worrying possibility.

In the UK while 'money management' has boomed, the rate of profit returned from manufacturing and industry has steadily declined (profit equals the return on capital invested). Investment in new buildings, manufacturing plant, training and research has tailed off and the British capitalists have survived by drastically cutting the workforce in the last twenty years. Now in 1992 the output of British manufacturing industry is below what it was in 1979. But because of the huge cuts in labour employed the bosses have managed to protect their profit, while their share of the market has declined greatly.

The outlook for British manufacturing industry is not good. Takeovers and asset stripping (selling off resources to raise cash) are helping to put off the day of reckoning. Eventually they are going to have to inflict further cuts on our standard of living through wage cuts (also called inflation) and cuts in State services. At the end of the day it is quite simple. When there is not enough in the pot to go around, the ruling class take what they want and leave us the scraps.

The capitalists also face a constant problem, coping with opposition from the working class and the peasants.

These then are the problems the international capitalist class face, their solution might include war, wage cuts, famine, green fascism and things which we cannot (or would not like to) foresee. But their solution will be dictated by their needs not ours.

● The Continuing Crisis of Capitalism - Revolution as the only Solution

To survive, and continue to generate a profit, business is compelled to continually expand, to produce more and more goods. This is due to the fierce and deadly competition created by the capitalist market place. However at no time can the capitalist consider the limits of the market. The idea is to increase their share of it and preferably take it over completely.

Therefore it is inevitable that there will be more of a particular product produced than can be sold at a profit on the market. But no business, industry or national economy exists in isolation, they are linked through the world market. In the past capitalists were able to avoid over-production by expanding beyond national boundaries into new markets i.e. those parts of the world that had pre-capitalist economies. This was achieved through colonialism, whereby the newly developed capitalist States literally seized political power by force from the native populations.

Despite attempts to head off the impending crisis, such as currency devaluations and increasing or decreasing State expenditure, a world recession did arrive in the early 1970's. Industrial production fell by 10% between 1974/75, international trade slumped and millions of workers lost their jobs. In fact since the late 1960's the world capitalist economy has been in a state of permanent crisis. The ruling class will claim, yes, there were recessions in 1974 and 1981 and 1991, but the periods in between have been periods of growth.

Yet if you look at it on a world scale the picture is quite different. All that happened was that the ruling class of the major capitalist countries found ways of hiding the recession. They've made others pay for the crisis; the lowest paid workers in their own countries and the destitute people in countries on the edge of capitalism, the so-called Third World. This they have achieved through the massive use of credit. In order to dispose of their goods the major industrialised countries have lent money on a huge scale.

To keep the illusion of economic prosperity, the major industrialised countries have given credit to less developed countries, so that they'll buy the goods from the West to keep the Western economies afloat. The debts are so large that they can never be paid off, giving the

Western lending countries even more control over the Third World economies. On the domestic front in countries like the UK, the late 1980's economic growth has been brought about by a consumer boom generated by easy access to credit; loans, charge cards, overdraughts etc. At the same time the USA, in particular, has tried to hold back the recession by embarking on a massive programme of arms production, financed by going into equally massive debt. The USA is the most indebted country in the world, with a domestic debt of $10 trillion and a foreign debt of $700 billion. If you add up the Third World's debts and that of the USA, it is easy to see that there isn't enough real money to repay them, or even pay off the interest on them.

All is not well in the international capitalist economy; maybe this system is really on its last legs. But you can bet that before the ruling class's time is up, they'll bleed us dry. The prospect of wage cuts, inflation, unemployment etc. all mean a massive deterioration in our living standards. A complete collapse of production, where output comes to a halt, is always on the cards, but is by no means inevitable. Unlike certain Lefties we do not believe in the 'natural' collapse of capitalism leading to a new classless society.

Capitalism will continue *AS LONG AS WE LET IT!* If we are to prevent a massive deterioration in our quality of life, we have only one option; to wage the class war, destroy capitalism once and for all and build a new world, a world of stability, freedom and prosperity for all.

For the working classes of the world the choice is simple. Revolution or barbarism. We choose revolution.

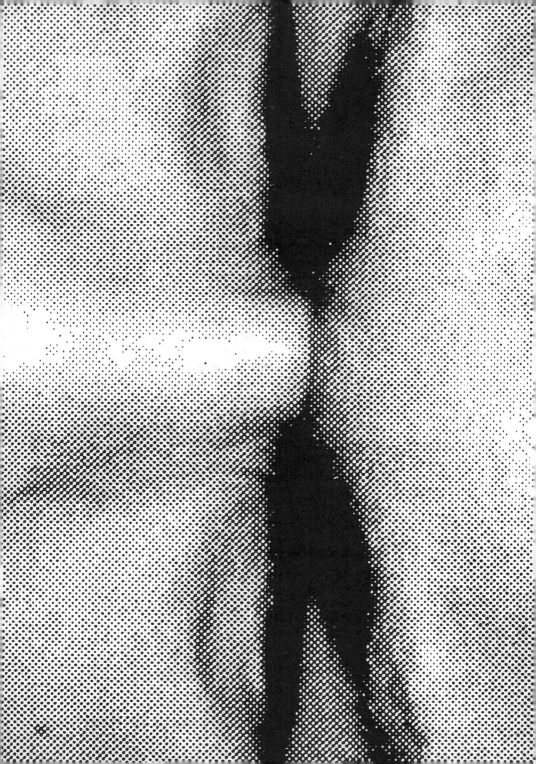

Chapter 2

The state

"You have by this time brought us under the heaviest burden and into the hardest yoke we ever knowed. We have counted up that we have gotten about sixty of us to every one of you; therefore should you govern, so many to one?"
Letter from the Norfolk Labourers to the Gentlemen of Ashill - 1816. *From "The making of the English Working Class." - E.P. Thompson*

Section Headings
- What is the State?
- What does the State do?
- Nationalism.
- Capitalism and the State.

● WHAT IS THE STATE?

Although capitalism is the dominant form of social organisation for production there are things that it cannot do on the basis of profit. Broadly speaking it cannot supply the civil organisation of society that it needs. This need of capitalism is met by something else, the State.

The State is the means by which a small minority control and dominate the huge majority in the interests of the ruling power in our society; the capitalists. To give an idea of the sizes of the classes involved the old often quoted statistics that over 84% of the wealth of our society is owned by 7% of the population still holds true and indicates how small the ruling class really is.

The State then, is that set of institutions and bodies through which government is exercised. For example, parliament, local government, ministries, civil service, police, education, church, tax collecting etc. The aim of this government is to control class conflict and regulate competition between the capitalists to ensure the smooth running of society. Adam Smith, the right-wing 18th century economic philosopher beloved of the 'New Right' in the UK and the USA was dead clear about the role of the State. Here is a statement of his that is not often quoted;

"Law and governments may be considered in this and indeed in every case as a combination of the rich to oppress the poor and preserve to themselves the inequality of the goods which would otherwise soon be destroyed by the attacks of the poor, who if not hindered by the government would soon reduce the others to an equality with themselves by open violence."

Here Smith hits the nail on the head. The main function of the State under capitalism is to enforce the law of private property and the right of the capitalist to buy and sell it despite the effect it has on our lives. Whether that property is land, food, sex, factories, houses - anything.

The State preceded capitalism and has always been a form of control and oppression in the interests of what ever ruling class is in power and of what ever economic system they choose to use e.g. the Roman ruling class in the Roman Empire had a highly developed State structure. The feudal States in Europe that existed before capitalism governed the people in the interest of another power or ruling group, the aristocracy. Often the church (of various kinds) was heavily involved. Every State seems to have to justify its own existence and authority with reference to the idea of a 'higher' or 'superior' power that is often a 'God' or it can be a philosophy that takes the place of a 'God' as with Marxist-Leninism in the so-called communist countries. While there is a State there will always be oppression.

● Religion and the State

As we have just mentioned the State always has to justify itself by reference to some superior force. We will go further than this now, and say that wherever you will find religion you will find the State. Why, you will ask? Our reasoning goes like this. Once you believe in divine beings or forces above humankind with superior power over our lives then you give up the right to control your own life yourself. If you look to divine guidance then you will look for the human representatives of that divine power on earth, or they will find you, whether they are guru's, wisemen, priests or Billy Graham. To them you will give your obedience. You will become a follower of the god or power you worship. Through this you will become a slave of the church and priests of your chosen god and through them you will become obedient to the State that they choose to bless. The point we are making here is that religion justifies and explains why one person should have power over another, which is the essence of the political power of the State. So, religion brings about the right conditions for the existence of the State. The Russian anarchist Michael Bakunin was absolutely clear about the negative effect of all religion;

"The idea of God, (or 'forces') implies the abdication of human reason and justice; it is the most decisive denial of human freedom and necessarily ends in the enslavement of humankind, both in theory and practice. If God is, then we are slaves; now, we can and must be free; then God does not exist. I defy anybody to avoid this circle, now, therefore, choose!"

"God and the State" - Michael Bakunin.

The established churches, such as the Church of England are an integral part of the State. In the UK the Church of England is part of the State machine with Bishops sitting in the House of Lords and the Privy Council. In times of crisis, like war or industrial and social unrest, the State will wheel out the priests. At crucial times in peoples lives the church is often involved, birth, marriage and death etc.

However, newer religions and churches have sprung up as a result of peoples disillusionment with the State and the conventional churches moral values. But these new religions generally channel peoples energy away from confrontation with the State into passive mystic nonsense. The new religions share all the same failings as the older religions.

● WHAT DOES THE STATE DO?

It delivers the kind of society that the capitalists need to keep doing business;

Military Force; it provides, at home and abroad, an armed force to protect capitalist interests. Capitalists do not have armies, States do. In the so-called communist countries the capitalist class is also in direct control of the State and its army which makes life a lot easier for them! When we say military force, in this category we can include special outfits like secret police, special branch, internal and external intelligence and security services such as MI5 and MI6, army intelligence, SAS etc. These organisations often have a close working relationship with directly funded capitalist organisations in the UK such as the Economic League, the Freemasons, the Adam Smith Institute and other right-wing think tanks and so on to form the networks that bind the ruling class together and through which power is exercised.

Political Stability; a situation where radical or revolutionary criticism of the ruling group is discouraged and prevented, by force if necessary. Instead discontent is channelled into harmless activities like petitions and elections. This harmless action is called reformism.

Education; this has three main roles; to justify and encourage acceptance of the economic and social order, in short to legitimise the status-quo; to organise young people's integration into society i.e. to make the most of the 'failures", and to supply the knowledge and skills to the workforce that capitalism needs.

Social Services; to alleviate the worst excesses of the capitalist system in order to aid stability.

Infrastructure; by this we mean the provision of the services the capitalists need for their society to work, for example; education, roads, communications and healthcare.

Law and Order; a legal force (the police and para-militaries) and a judicial system (the courts and judges), that protects the capitalists

from those whom they exploit and that controls the activities of the lower classes.

How the State Works in Practice

Every State has a group of unelected permanent managers and bureaucrats who are the elite of the civil service and a very powerful group in their own right, e.g. the cabinet secretary, the secretary to the treasury, secretaries to ministries and the chief executives of local authorities.

Then there are the politicians who compete to control the State machine and its managers. These politicians represent different groups or cliques in the capitalist camp. Their ability to control the State machine depends on the strength of the power group they represent.

The condition for us to have a right to vote in this competition is that all the candidates are on the boss's side.

Democracy

The British State is supposed to be controlled by the politicians and the politicians elected by us. This, we are told, allows us through the ballot box to change things. So why does the State act in the interests of the ruling class regardless of whoever is in power - Labour, Tory or Liberal? It is because to function and succeed politicians and their parties are ultimately controlled by the capitalists and the States own permanent unelected officials. Lets look at the activities of these two groups.

The Capitalists and the State

Groups that speak for the capitalists interests, like the Confederation of British Industry (CBI) and the City of London (also increasingly international finance) put forward their requirements to the politicians and their parties and watch closely for their response. If they are ignored the offending politicians and political parties are ridiculed and attacked, through the capitalist propaganda media machine of the newspapers, TV, radio, advertising etc. Many of the political parties rely for their funding from rich backers which can be used to exert pressure.

● The State Officials and Managers

The State is a huge machine containing many powerful non-elected officials. Elected politicians are relatively small in number and wrapped up in public relations and electioneering work a lot of the time. This leaves them relying very heavily on the advice they receive from the State officials, or rather the advice these officials see fit to give them. Challenging this unelected power group would be very time consuming and very difficult, not surprisingly politicians don't do so very often. The fact is that the State has a life of its own separate from the elected politicians.

In practice the capitalists, the politicians and the State officials have the same values and objectives, most of the time. In the UK most of these people will have gone to similar schools and universities. Together they constitute the bulk of the ruling class *(see Chapter Three on class)* and keep in close touch with each other through official and unofficial means. Factions within this class come into conflict in pursuing their own objectives but for the most part this is handled internally through their own social networks and organisations, only occasionally do the differences surface in court or the newspapers. As it exists, democracy is most definitely an illusion. It fools us into thinking we can change things through the vote. It also give us figure heads to blame for our difficulties such as this or that Party or politician. The purpose is to make us identify with the State and its values and channel our discontent into safe, legal activities that will absorb all our energy.

Instead of the chance of voting every four years or so for one of the bosses candidates we aspire to a society where people represent themselves and their needs directly to each other. This has all been done before in Russia, Germany, Spain and Hungary for example. By local, regional and international assemblies of people, workers councils and Soviets with the use of immediately recallable delegates to represent groups of people all operating within a federal structure i.e. independent groups sharing common aims and values.

We see the new, so-called, 'democracy' movements of Eastern Europe as a futile attempt to ape Western methods of government and as the expression of a politically ambitious middle class and a small group of frustrated capitalists. Equally we see the attempt by the Left in the UK to vote 'radical' MP's into parliament as useless. While we understand peoples desires for a better way of life, parliamentary style representative 'democracy' is not the means to achieve it. Why do we take this view? Firstly, because parliament is not where the decisive power lies within this society and secondly, if the ruling class were actually threatened by an elected government they would remove it. This 'removal' can take two forms; by force as with the socialist government of Allende in Chile in 1973, or by intrigue as with the Labour government of Wilson in the UK in 1974-76.

Genuine popular uprisings against capitalism and the State are crushed without mercy. For example Russia 1905, Germany 1919, Spain 1937, Hungary 1956 and many more. Faced with a determined revolt international capitalists will often act as one, through the means of finance and the military force of nation-states.

● Military Adventures

The military force of the State is used by capitalists in competition with each other to defend or further their own interests. Politicians and State managers will also use military force to further their own ambitions. The Falklands/Malvinas war certainly saved Thatcher and Co. from a humiliating election defeat by whipping up a frenzy of nationalist patriotism at a time when they were presiding over massive job losses and were one of the most unpopular governments ever in the history of the UK. In 1991 the Gulf War secured long term oil-supplies for the First World.

● Regulation

The State can also act to regulate the activities of individual capitalists who could threaten stability and upset the dominant interests within the ruling class. For example the banks are only able to function under license from the State. There are also a whole range of regulations and guidelines governing manufacture, distribution and employment in Britain. This is primarily in the interest of stability and represents the deals that capitalism has had to do with the working class in Britain to keep going, deals that are negotiated through the State machine by the labour movement.

The British trade unions are crucial to this role of regulation, stability and control and because of this you will find union officials on many committees. In advanced capitalist countries like the UK capitalism cannot function without the help of the unions.

● NATIONALISM

This is the process where the ruling class try to get the working class to identify with the State and its values. To achieve this identification racism, religion and patriotism are often used. Nationalism can be present where a new State is in the process of being formed against the will of an occupying State, as in Northern Ireland, Palestine and the republics of the old USSR.

● British Nationalism

The British working class identify strongly with their State and as such are very nationalistic. The heart of this 'British' nationalism is really English and grows from the fact that the British State is really still identified with an English identity. Two socialist historians comment;

"Englishness - as nationalism at home, and imperialism abroad - permeates the social power of the State, enormously enhancing its legitimacy through a systematic practice of identification."

From "The Great Arch" by Corrigan and Sayer.

The English are an extreme example of nationalism, having had their original culture and identity largely destroyed with the start of capitalism and the industrial revolution. English national identity was largely remade in the late 19th century with the Royal family at the centre, they had previously been spat at when they dared venture on the streets! A lot of the English do not even realise it, it is so deeply conditioned that many cannot see what the Irish are complaining about, or the Scots or before them the Indians and Africans! As a Welsh socialist historian pointed out,

"It is as if a really secure nationalism (i.e. English), already in possession of its own nation-state, does not see itself as 'nationalist' at all",

Raymond Williams.

The British State is not as secure as it once was, it is facing increasing resistance from within, (Northern Ireland, Scotland, Wales and even different regions of England). Politically ambitious sections of the middle and upper classes are often involved in drawing up schemes for local devolution etc. from which they will benefit of course.

● Other People's Nationalism - Identity

However, we have no wish to deny or limit the diversity of different peoples and their cultures. But the nation-state is not the best expression for this identity. We look forward to a world without frontiers. All States are artificial creations, a line on a map does not define a people but it does define a piece of property which is what a nation-state is all about.

Meanwhile, the domination and exploitation of groups of people and their lands by strong nation-states such as the USA, USSR, UK etc., causes much suffering through physical and economic repression, and denial of native identity and culture. This experience is real. The Irish, Palestinians, Kurds, East Timorese etc. are not imagining what is happening to them. They're being oppressed by another country. This brutal process is at the heart of imperialism and takes many forms. Sometimes direct occupation such as Britain in Northern Ireland or using a puppet native government, as in some African countries, to exploit the local economy in the interests of international capitalism (called Neo-colonialism.) Either way resistance makes itself felt. This resistance can be channelled into aspirations to form an 'independent' nation free of the outside oppressor. This approach is naturally promoted by the 'local' middle and upper classes who have the most to gain from such independence. While we agree with the removal of such imperial and colonial oppression we argue and fight against the 'local' oppression waiting in the wings to take over.

● The Response of the British Left to Imperialism

Trotsky once said the British Left love a revolution as long as it's a thousand miles away. This is very true. Their response is either complete support for every national liberation movement or complete rejection of them all for being backward. This is not good enough.

● Fighting Back

Those at the sharp end of the oppression of imperialism and colonialism often have little choice but to fight back in whatever way they can. People in the UK and similar countries whose governments are responsible for the most brutal acts in places like Ireland and the Palestine often have difficulty in understanding the actions of those fighting against 'their' government. This is hardly surprising as most of us in the UK have no experience of organised murder, torture and terror. It's this real experience at the hands of the British State that leads people to join the IRA and similar republican organisations.

What we must understand is that in the face of often brutal oppression nationalism gives working class people something. This 'something' is identity, pride, a feeling of community and solidarity and of course physical self-defence. We need to combat capitalism and its nationalism with something as strong i.e. with our own identity, pride, community, solidarity, history, culture and the inspiration of the international working class. To achieve this effectively will require courage and determination. To challenge nationalist ideas means doing more than saying that they are bad, we must prove that fighting for our class is better than fighting for a country.

To those people involved in often desperate struggles against imperialism we need to speak as equals with some respect for their struggle and sacrifices, in the same way as we seek to speak to our class at 'home'. That means we have to match their courage and determination. Then we will be in a position to criticise effectively the negative and reactionary elements in their nationalist movements, and we will be able to do so if we are seen to be as hard on our own home-grown British nationalism as their's. Unless we can do this we will suffer the same fate as much of the Russian anarchist movement, who sat in their intellectual circles waiting for a 'pure' social movement to form before they would condescend to get involved. They rejected much of the Russian revolution out of hand and the Ukrainian anarchist insurgents as merely 'nationalists'. We wonder how many of the modern anarchists are set to repeat this miserable mistake where arrogance is only exceeded by ignorance. This obviously leads on to the question of Northern Ireland. *Please refer to the Appendix for our views on this matter.*

● CAPITALISM AND THE STATE

In the so-called advanced capitalist countries of the world like the UK and France, the State plays a crucial role. In these countries the changes brought about by the 'Restructuring of Capital', mentioned in Chapter One, have made great demands on the State as the lower classes are forced to accept cuts in living standards. The State's response has been a three fold attack. Firstly, there has been an intense and sophisticated propaganda campaign orchestrated by politicians through the media. The main thrust of this campaign has been to minimise or deny the existence of class and to transfer the blame for unemployment and poverty onto the individual. Phrases like; "Get On Yer Bike" and "Scrounger", are still ringing in our ears from these campaigns of the 1970's and 80's. Secondly, the steady dismantling of the welfare state to keep workers tied to their jobs and accept lower wages - by the removal of the safety net and cushion of welfare benefits, especially unemployment benefits. Thirdly, the State's strategy of rolling-back the powers of the organisations that represent and control the working class in the workplaces; the unions. This has now largely been achieved.

● Mass Culture and the State

It is worth saying here that there are two branches of enterprise that work closely with the State from the point of view of social control; the media and the advertising companies with their related off shoots such as research and public relations. The huge growth in these areas in the late 20th century shows how capitalism has become more bureacratised and the extent that it has to plan ahead just to survive. It also shows how important the creation and control of so-called popular culture is now in the advanced capitalist countries. During the 1991 Gulf War the UK government employed no less than four public relations companies to 'market' the war.

● The Carrot and the Stick

In the advanced capitalist countries with their new industries and growing service sectors, it is absolutely vital that the workforce are self-motivated. Brutal coercion will not programme computers, make high-tech weapons, or inspire white collar workers to administer pension funds or insurance schemes. Nor will it force builders to build or drivers to drive. No, for advanced capitalism to work effectively, the workforce has to identify and agree with the aims and values of the capitalists and they must feel involved in things, without this they will not be motivated. These ideas and values are called 'bourgeois ideology' by the Left.

● The Carrot

Things are made easier for the capitalists in these countries because the working class benefit materially from the international position that 'their' country occupies. Some (but not most) working class people can do quite well in terms of material benefits, in almost a quite random way (called the "bingo effect") depending on where they work or where they live. Some examples; until recently some work, like printing, was highly paid because of the workplace organisation and the wealth of the employers. On Fleet Street, printers used to be paid more than some of the management! More dramatically, people were buying their council houses in South East England for say £20,000 and were able to sell a couple of years later in the 'boom' of the late 1980's for over £100,000! The "bingo effect" can only apply to a few but makes a powerful impression on the rest of us - adding to the idea that it is possible to 'make it'. It is part of the carrot that is offered to us.

● The Stick

Of course coercion of an economic kind is there. If the boredom, stupidity or low pay of work pisses people off, then the alternative is no work and no pay and the prospect of sliding down the social scale to the bottom of society. To keep people going to work in the morning and to stop those at the bottom from revolting, modern capitalism and the State have to fill people's minds with the 'right' ideas, and deny the validity of those ideas that question the status-quo. They do this by the means of the media and mass culture.

This task of social control started in the 1700's for the capitalist. Now it is an enormous job, every day the ruling class has to explain and justify the present situation to us, or re-invent the world as some wit has remarked. If they stop or reduce the pressure our society will disintegrate under the weight of its own contradictions. This is the role of bourgeois ideology; to keep the whole manure-heap from collapsing, and is in a large measure what the middle class are employed to do. These ideas, and the social relations of capitalism seem strong but they are also brittle and can shatter under a sudden blow from our class.

● The State - Conclusions

The power of the State lies in the hands of the capitalists because they control it. The government exists to protect the existing social order and class system. Therefore the primary duty of the State is the enforcement of property laws and protection of privileges associated with ownership. The principal freedom the capitalists want to protect is the freedom to buy and sell which is at the heart of their society. If at any time this set-up is seriously threatened by the working class the government will respond by force of arms.

The State represents the dominant views and values within the ruling class, not one or two individuals. In a country like the UK one of its most important jobs is to promote these views and values through education, religion and the media. Lastly, there is always the risk that a small group can mount an attempt to gain control of the State. For example a fascist coup or Lenin inspired communists of the Bolshevik type.

Chapter 3

Class

"The Working Class? They're no problem. I can buy one half to kill the other half!"

J.P. Morgan - *American Banker 1991*

Section Headings
● Introduction.
● Outline of the Class Structure in Britain.
● The Working Class - Political Divisions.
● The Working Class - Economic Divisions.
● Summing up on Class.

● INTRODUCTION

So far we have covered capitalism and the State and shown how these two forces have produced the kind of society we live in. As capitalism represents exploitation and the State domination then it is hardly surprising that the society they have produced is split into different categories or classes of people who occupy a position or status by virtue of their relation to capitalism and the State. In this chapter on class we get down to the business of applying to society what we have found out about capitalism and the State. As you might expect, we have a lot to say on the subject of class.

● Class Structure

The traditional view of the class division of society still holds true, this sees three main divisions;
● The ruling class; at the top, composed of the capitalists and State managers.
● The middle class; in the middle, composed of the 'middle management' of capitalism and the State.
● The working class; they are the people who are exploited and dominated by the other two classes. They consist of those who live and work in the industrialised world, and those who live and work in parts of the world that are not very industrialised, consisting of rural

workers and farmers; called peasants. We see these rural workers as belonging to the same class, the oppressed. The Left traditionally looks upon them as reactionary and a problem, a view we do not share, and a view that history shows is nonsense (as in Spain, Russia, Haiti, Jamaica, The Ukraine, China, Mexico, South America, etc.) This then is the broad outline of the class structure. It will be useful to try and fill in a bit more detail in this picture of the class system, in the UK.

● OUTLINE OF THE CLASS STRUCTURE IN BRITAIN

Please note - the size of the classes quoted here have been derived from the 1981 census returns. The State has lists of social classes and socio-economic groups. Both are defined by occupation. Their allocation of occupation to class and socio-economic group does not always agree with our conception of class. For instance much of the white collar work we would regard to be working class they consider to be middle class, hence the assertion recently by some British politicians that the working class is disappearing.

● The Ruling Class

SIZE; absolute maximum of about 5% (probably much less) of population = approx. 2.75 million people.

IDENTITY; examples of capitalists; owners of companies and major shareholders, executive and managing directors of the top British companies, bankers, senior managers of investment and insurance companies, stockbrokers, property and landowners, not forgetting the royals and other aristocrats who pervade all the top levels of British society.

Examples of state managers; top civil service managers in national and local government, cabinet ministers, high court judges and law lords, members of the privy council, staff officers of the armed forces, police chiefs, high level advisors such as some economists and top academics such as Oxbridge dons, and of course church leaders.

FUNCTION; to maintain their own and their class's domination over society. Their favourite method is 'divide and rule'; notably setting whites against blacks and other races against each other, called racism; setting men against women, called sexism and setting worker against worker. Of course these divisions do not apply to the ruling class. They are intended only for working class consumption. The morals, rules and laws of the ruling class do not apply to themselves, their purpose is to keep us in our place. The strategy of the ruling class is to keep their class united and others divided.

● The ruling classes compete fiercely with each other for markets, resources and political power. War between nation-states and civil war is often the result.

ORIGINS; many are born into the class in Britain but in other countries they tend to come from all sections of society.

● The Middle Class

SIZE; about 20% of population = approx. 11 million people.

IDENTITY; examples of 'professional' people who work for capitalism and the State; J.P.'s, journalists, doctors, officers in the armed forces, researchers; management: in manufacture, sales, distribution and service industries; small employers (i.e. small capitalists), social workers, vicars and priests, teachers, etc.

FUNCTION; to manage the working class in the interests of the ruling class. To ensure the smooth running of capitalist society. To watch out for potential crisis in capitalism and devise avoiding action. To manufacture 'culture', both high and popular: including pop music, fashion, philosophy, opera and TV.

● To provide technical skills for capitalism and the State in the realm of production and especially management. A section of the middle class employed by the State form what has been nicknamed 'the mandarin class' (named after the old Chinese Imperial civil service who formed a powerful group in their own right). Then there are the 'failed mandarins' often of a Lefty persuasion who content themselves with creating small time job opportunities in local government to do 'good works' in an attempt to 'save' the working class.

● To research into different methods of production and social organisation for instance 'green' economics or 'communes'. To promote ideas that keep us divided like racism and sexism by means of the media, education and religion that they control. To explain and justify the existing organisation of society. To divert our energy into harmless activity that is called reformism e.g. Greenpeace, CND, feminism, trades unions - activities which at best will only modify your misery and will not do anything to change the fundamental nature of society.

● The Working Class

SIZE; about 75% of the population = approx. 41.25 million people.

IDENTITY; the briefest way of describing our class is to say they are everyone who is not in the middle and ruling classes! This is not just a smart arse remark. In general the working class are people who live by their labour (even the dole can be seen as a 'wage' - its the deal the State strikes with us to prevent unrest by the unemployed); the ownership of property that generates wealth is a dividing line. If you have enough property or money not to have to work then you are not working class. The other component of class identity is 'social power'. The working classes do not have power. They are the ones who are told what to do. As a class we are defined by the activities of capitalism and the State, and the two classes that benefit most from the status-quo; the ruling class and the middle class.

THE WORKING CLASSES ARE DEFINED NOT BY WHAT THEY DO BUT BY WHAT IS DONE TO THEM. THEY ARE THE CREATION OF CAPITALISM. This is not to say that we are powerless, far from it. Huge amounts of effort and money are devoted to keeping us in our place. The working class are the only people capable of destroying

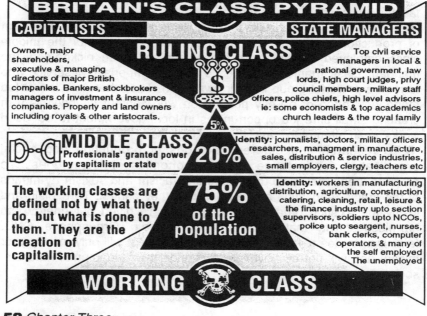

BRITAIN'S CLASS PYRAMID

CAPITALISTS

Owners, major shareholders, executive & managing directors of major British companies. Bankers, stockbrokers managers of investment & insurance companies. Property and land owners including royals & other aristocrats.

RULING CLASS

STATE MANAGERS

Top civil service managers in local & national government, law lords, high court judges, privy council members, military staff officers, police chiefs, high level advisors ie: some economists & top academics church leaders & the royal family

5%

MIDDLE CLASS
'Proffesionals' granted power by capitalism or state

20%

Identity: journalists, doctors, military officers researchers, managment in manufacture, sales, distribution & service industries, small employers, clergy, teachers etc

The working classes are defined not by what they do, but what is done to them. They are the creation of capitalism.

75%
of the population

Identity: workers in manufacturing distribution, agriculture, construction catering, cleaning, retail, leisure & the finance industry upto section supervisors, soldiers upto NCOs, police upto seargent, nurses, bank clerks, computer operators & many of the self employed The unemployed

WORKING   CLASS

capitalism and the State, and building a better world for everyone. Because our work is at the centre of everyday practical economic activity in capitalism it would be fair to say it all hinges around whether we want to 'play the game'.

IDENTITY; examples; factory workers, distribution workers in road, rail, air and sea, retail workers in shops, construction and building, service industries such as leisure, cleaning, catering and the finance industry up to section supervisors. Agricultural workers, workers in the chemicals, steel, drugs, coal, electronics, engineering industries, many of the self-employed e.g. brickies, plasterers, truck drivers etc., nurses (over 500,000 - the biggest single work group), secretaries, bank clerks, computer operators, soldiers up to NCO level, the unemployed, the poor, the destitute - those of no property.

● The Question of Working Class Identity

The working class has it's identity questioned and attacked from the cradle to the grave. Instead of their obvious and real identity, together with their real need for mutual solidarity, they are offered a warped image of themselves. This image is deferential to their 'betters' and a patriotic pride in the State (the UK) and Royalty. Their self confidence is comprehensively attacked by education, religion and the media. Superstitious and bigoted ideas are encouraged at every opportunity.

The people who do this to us (the middle class) then have the cheek to moan about how awful we are! For instance our young men are encouraged to be aggressive and competitive and are praised as patriots when they go to fight for their masters in Ireland, Argentina and Iraq. Yet when they swagger down the street on Saturday nights they are 'louts' or worse according to what paper you read.

If you look at the media in the UK you will find that the working class are allowed only three kinds of image and are encouraged to look at themselves in the following ways;

●The honest, loyal, hard working, good hearted citizen.

●The stupid and the misguided, to be patronised.

●The rest, who are portrayed as scum, animals and evil who are constantly to be put in their place; who are to be shot down like dogs when the need arises.

Into this third category the media will shuffle anybody that stands up against injustice and oppression e.g. strikers, prisoners, gays, blacks, rioters, etc. and us. All we can say is that we are in good company!

We are offered a way of life by our rulers that is 'normal'. In this false world of 'normal', patriotism is considered good when in fact all it represents is loyalty to our rulers. Parochialism, i.e. being concerned with only what happens in your own small corner of the world, is encouraged at every turn from the 'Little Englander' attitudes of the southern counties of England, to the 'Tyke Nationalism' of Yorkshire and the sentimental myths surrounding Scottish nationalism. Ignorance and racism are elevated to virtues in the 'normal' outlook and re-inforced at every opportunity by the media and advertising. Even the way we speak becomes a way of assigning class identity and privilege in our society. BBC English has the police jumping through hoops!

● Function of the Working Class

Exploited; to produce goods and services for the capitalists in return for a wage. To buy back what we produce, (whether we need it or not!) To act as a market for capitalism. In short to be exploited.

Dominated; to be ordered around by the State's laws, police and the bosses rules; to be the target for vile political campaigns aimed at splitting and antagonising our class from each other e.g. young and old, workers and unemployed, black and white, men and women, gays and heterosexuals, parents and kids.

Exterminated; to be the cannon fodder in the military adventures of their governments, yet the middle and upper class express horror at the class they have helped create as if it has nothing to do with them. Yes we are wild and brutal at times - oppression does not necessarily make you a nice person.

● Class Structure - General Points

In general there are two main components that give you your place in the class system, *WEALTH* and *SOCIAL POWER*. Confused? If there is any doubt in placing someone in class terms then social power is definitely the deciding factor.

● THE WORKING CLASS - POLITICAL DIVISIONS

This is a good time to talk about the main divisions that afflict our class and keep us weak. The main divisions are nationalism, racism, sexism, and anti-gay bigotry. We are not born like this. It is an artificial state of affairs and can be changed. In fact we have a strong tendency to unity and solidarity because daily around the world our class shares the same experiences; essentially to be bossed around (dominated) and ripped off (exploited). In fact we have so much in common and so much to gain from coming together that it is obvious to those that rule us that we must be stopped from doing so at all costs.

Their method is the tried and tested one of 'divide and rule'. They use nationalism, sexism, racism, religion and hatred of gays to turn us against each other. Education, religion, culture, the media and advertising are the carriers of these poisonous ideas. As each generation gets battered down by this process they tend to bring their kids up the same way. Yet not all of us get fooled and sometimes in the course of struggles such as strikes and wars we get to see what is really going on in this world. This is what the ruling class dread. They know that solidarity and ideas can spread like wildfire amongst us. The pressure from us toward unity is so strong that the ruling class has to devote lots of time, energy and money to keeping our heads full of nonsense. They employ some of the middle class to do this for them.

● Religion

This is much more important than many of us in the UK at first realise. We will concentrate here on Christianity, the 'official' religion of the British State, but much of what follows applies to all religions. Much of what we say here follows on from the points made about the relation between religion and the State in Chapter Two.

Throughout history, the growth and control of organised religions has been a perversion of natural and social needs that people have felt: the hunger to explain ourselves, how we relate to each other and the world, and the curiosity about where we come from. This is a positive and useful inquisitiveness that we all have.

The religious leaders have worked hand in hand with the capitalists, the State and politicians to exercise moral, social, and political control over the world's working classes. This is all to keep themselves in mystical positions of power by forcing social and religious beliefs upon us, (often at the point of death; look at the missionary work in the early days of capitalist imperialism). In the UK many of us are supposed to believe in the official religion of Christianity. We are told that Christ was a guy who knocked around 2000 years ago, was born by a woman

who never had sex with a man, worked magic tricks, got crucified, rose from the dead and went to a place called heaven where everything is nice. Come on! Pull the other one! We are told that this is the "true faith" and that other religions such as Islam, Buddhism, Taoism etc. are 'backward', which is a laugh.

● Catholicism

The Catholic Church is a massive multinational company, a land owner with the richest city (the Vatican) in the world as the jewel in its rotten crown. The majority of the Catholics in the world are working class and peasants, living in poverty. But they are expected to give, and live, for the greater glory of a God whose spokesman on earth is the Pope, a close friend of some of the most right-wing regimes in the world, and who vindictively opposes both contraception and abortion, condemning many women to poverty and ill health.

● Church of England

These religious leaders regularly change their ideas to hang on to their followers. In the 1950's Rock and Roll was seen by most Christian 'thinkers' as "the Devil's Music". But now in 1992 the present Archbishop of Canterbury says he loves pop music in an effort to attract young people back to his church. The same church, the Church of England, is officially part of the government of this country, and regularly blesses weapons of mass destruction and justifies the brutality of British forces in Northern Ireland. This church owns thousands of empty properties and acres of land yet does nothing about homelessness.

Both Protestantism and Catholicism massacred untold numbers of women in the Middle Ages in Europe as they extended their spiritual and physical empires. Their hatred of and discrimination against women has left a scar on our class in the form of sexism from this era. We have not forgotten.

All religions benefit by encouraging distrust and bigotry between different peoples such as racism. This has the effect of binding their followers more closely to the church (the sectarianism in Northern Ireland is actually good for the churches on both sides). Again the early history of colonialism is instructive. Many Christian religious leaders pronounced that the 'natives' were not human, had no soul and so it was OK to kill and enslave them as they were little more than animals!

Just as capitalism is a small number of people controlling what we have and how much we have to work to get it, organised religion means God's bosses seek to socially control us.

In the Spanish Revolution of the 1930's some of the peasants who had lived in squalor and ignorance under the rule of the Catholic Church for centuries showed what they thought of their spiritual leaders. They shot every Nun and Priest they could find and when they ran out of live ones they went to the graveyards and dug up the dead ones and shot them too! Not content with this, in several places statues of Christ were taken down from the walls of the churches and 'He' was tried for his crimes against the people.

After being sentenced to death the statue was taken in front of a firing squad, shot and then buried. Notices were then posted around some villages announcing that the leader of the gang (the Church) responsible for so much physical and emotional suffering amongst the peasants had been caught and executed. The notice added that this time Christ was not coming back!

This brilliant piece of working class propaganda sets very well the right tone for dealing with religion.

● Racism

The splitting up of people along the lines of where they come from, or the colour of their skin is dead useful at keeping the working class weak. But racism does not just attempt to create a division in the working class, its aim is to make sections of the working class support and collaborate with the ruling class. Racism, by creating an illusion that there is some sort of natural unity between members of the same ethnic group disguises the real nature of class conflict within capitalism. Nationalism functions in much the same way, as was described in Chapter Two.

In this way class consciousness is replaced with race consciousness. That is, when sections of the working class believe they have more in common with their rulers than other sections of their class. Class issues get turned into race issues as the media, the State and the ruling class scapegoat black sections of the working class for problems created by the capitalist system, like unemployment. Please note that when we say 'black' we mean all non-white people in this country.

What the white working class get out of racism is a sense of superiority and identity and the feeling of being better treated by the State and the bosses. While most of this is an illusion it is a powerful illusion. The only sense of power allowed the working class in this society is when they crap on someone else. There is a defined pecking order and at the bottom are black women.

Racism in Britain has caused the isolation of many ethnic groups. The response to this treatment on a local and national level has been the setting up of black political organisations. This has been a necessary step, due to the crippling effect of racism on the British white working class. While we welcome such initiatives we push for a wider class consciousness within these movements.

● Sexism

The importance of this division to our class is reflected here in the length devoted to it. Sexism means the oppression and putting down of women just because we are women, implying we are of lesser importance than men. All women experience this to varying degrees according to what class they live in. While this division predates capitalism and came from religion, it has been used by capitalists for their own ends, working in partnership with the State to justify the oppression of women by men. Exploiting this sexual division enables them to keep the cost of producing future generations of workers down by getting free childcare and family maintenance. Whether a person is female or male should be of no importance. Biological differences are irrelevant. The fact that our sex is used to decide our future life opportunities is a social and political division.

Sexism like racism, is a form of prejudice promoted by those in power, via the media, legislation and 'popular' commercial culture. Its purpose is to keep the working class divided. The effect of this discrimination is to exclude us from the arena of public life i.e. work, politics, business, trade unions, the media and anything which can influence public opinion in a big way. By these means women become 'non' people, not worth consulting with.

"The consistency and completeness, over the centuries, of the exclusion and subordination of women has no real parallel in the experience of any other social group, and nowhere is it clearer how central a problem the 'State' remains if human capacities are ever to be fully realised."

"The Great Arch" (notes on the making of the English ruling class)- Corrigan and Sayer.

This exclusion from public life applies to all but the lucky or the rich. On a practical level the availability of childcare is crucial for women to take part in public life, either in paid work, or involvement in community groups, trade unions or politics. Yet this is treated as a very minor side issue, relegated to the interests of the so-called 'loony left' by the likes of the tabloid newspapers.

Women are seen and valued in terms of their body. It is important to live up to expectations of attractiveness. A multi-billion pound industry caters for this, reinforcing the idea of looking good. By skilful marketing and manipulation women are encouraged to spend vast sums of money on cosmetics, clothes, slimming products, health clubs, exercise classes etc. This fascination with the body-beautiful is connected to sexuality and both are used to sell anything; cars, holidays, clothing, food, etc. We are presented with a series of impossible roles and images to live up to, many of which contradict each other such as the virgin, the whore, the mother, the worker, the career woman, the slim 'object of desire' and so on. All this social conditioning which we receive via the family, education, religion, the media and various State institutions is intended to get us to accept a second rate status in life. It is 'our duty' to accept these limitations we are told, and as for imagining things could be a whole lot better...

● Changes

The various phases of womens political movements from the 1880's onwards has had some impact in changing public attitudes about women, and introducing women to political life, increasing womens influence and representation. It has done better in the area of health care. The development of effective contraception and the legalisation of abortion has helped to improve maternal health and lowered mortality rates. Control over our own fertility, being able to decide if and when we have children and how many, is a major gain in womens lives. Concerns about political, economic and social rights are meaningless if you have ten children to look after.

The other major change is the large increase in the numbers of women working outside the home. The limited economic independence this created has brought a certain amount of freedom with it. In capitalism if you have no income of your own your options are severely limited as anyone on long term welfare benefits will tell you.

Employment outside the home is no longer the issue it was in the 1950's when the ruling class propaganda pushed the ideas that a "womens place is in the home". Of course in times of crisis and war there has been no problem in creating nurseries for children to enable women to work. This is one of the roles that women fulfil in capitalism to act as a "reserve army of labour" to be called on as and when the need arises. As the film "Rosie the Riveter" showed, women were forced back into the home after the Second World War to make room for the men returning from the armed forces, similar events happened in the First World War as well. A womans place is wherever the ruling class seem to think they need us! One minute we are all supposed to be career women; the next we are all supposed to be meek wives at home. The 'back to the home' trick maybe wheeled out again as the recession deepens in the 1990's.

The jobs women do now are still lower paid and lower status despite equal pay legislation. Relative to men, women earn two thirds of the average male wage and are concentrated at the lower levels of the workforce pecking order. Since the 1960's most women work,

often on a part-time basis until their children are older. Much of this is in work that is part time or temporary, and often in non-unionised and low-paid sectors.

● The Present

The sexual division of labour also puts pressure on men, mainly to be breadwinners. They need to be ambitious, to compete and to win. With aggressiveness not far behind. This is the economic basis of what is, at present, the male identity. This identity is centred around the job they do. Without this a man has no status and no useful role to play in society as it is currently structured. Men are certainly not encouraged to show interest in home based activities, as this is, in effect, the womans workplace, and since when has being a full time housewife been a high-status occupation? These different attitudes and lifestyles distort the relationships between women and men. Both lose out, and there is much unhappiness, which while not formally spoken about, shows itself in disastrous relationships, marriages or domestic violence. Now in some parts of the UK it is the women who make up the bulk of the workforce due to male unemployment caused by the capitalists restructuring of the 1970's and 80's. This is another ingredient in the tensions between men and women.

The principle that we should be able to support ourselves and not need the long term financial support of a man is attractive in theory. However while we are seen as the primary carers of children, elderly parents and disabled relatives, our position in the workplace is regarded as secondary to our work as mothers and wives or girlfriends (a heterosexual relationship is assumed here). This is used to justify lower wages, as it is assumed we are economically and socially dependant and not people in our right.

The idea that childcare should be more equally shared between the sexes is a good one, but in practice women find themselves working the double shift. Having worked during the day, we come home and start on round two; the washing, ironing, cooking and looking after the children. There is no direct male equivalent. When men have had enough, they can go down the pub etc. A woman doesn't have the same option, since firstly children are not welcome and secondly, pubs are a male environment in which an unaccompanied woman is seen as 'fair game' to be 'picked up'. Its hard to round up female friends for a night out due to all their own commitments. It is of course easier for young unattached women - until they 'settle down' that is.

The social security system, along with that other wonderful social institution, marriage; where for instance the married couples tax allowance (or dole) is only payable to the man, are good examples of institutionalised sexism. Men do not need to concern themselves about the cohabitation rules which cut women off from any welfare benefits in their own right and force them towards dependence on a man. Imagine what having no income of your own does to your self confidence or sense of identity in a society built around money.

● Objectives and the Future

The objectives of equality for women can only be achieved as part of a wider social revolution (very true in respect of how family responsibilities regarding childcare are concerned).

It needs to be recognised that women will need to organise separately at certain stages of the class struggle. This is vital in order to overcome the discrimination that we face. Its not just lack of childcare that holds us back but the pressure involved in working in groups made up of mainly men and thus mostly concerned about things of interest to men. Women need their own organisations as well, to gain the necessary experience to deal with public life and represent our interests, so that we can participate in events, contributing actively to the fight of our class. What is being proposed is not female separatism, which is a safe haven for the middle class feminist, but the means to enable women to play their part in the wider class struggle, and avoid becoming marginalised, as has happened in other revolutions. While it is true that the women's or 'feminist' movement (the latter term has become a word of abuse), has mainly benefited middle class women who dominate it, this does not mean that women do not need their own organisations. It is not a choice of class struggle or womens liberation, it is both. One cannot happen without the other.

The only way working class women will get a better deal is through our own efforts, no one else will do it for us. When we start to take control of our lives, and get out of the habit of being passive and waiting for permission or approval from others before doing anything, we gain confidence just by getting on and doing things. That is when we realise how well we have been fooled.

We need to recognise that we have the right and the need to determine our own lives ourselves and not let others constantly do this for us. Equally it is for us to take action, to achieve a better way of life and not expect it to be handed to us on a plate. This will involve struggle and radical change, initially in the area of how we think and feel about ourselves and by working in the wider social movement.

As working class women our voice and identity has been denied throughout history. Any revolutionary organisation that denies or plays down the importance of women's freedom is useless to the struggle to build a better world.

● Sexuality

Another key way of keeping us divided is by laying down the rules on with who, and how, we should love or have sex with.

● Men and Women

Relations between men and women (heterosexual relationships) are a constant source of tension and conflict. Sexuality is the virtual monopoly of men, for men. This male dominance has led to all sorts of double standards, hypocrisy and contradictions. Promiscuity in men is supposed to be a sign of natural virility; in women it means they are branded a 'whore', 'slag' or 'tart'.

Capitalist society in general is filled with all sorts of hypocrisy. On the one hand the sexual moralists, like Mary Whitehouse and the churches, are given a free hand to spout their guilt-ridden nonsense which tries to deny any form of pleasure from sex and insist that sex is only legitimate within the confines of marriage and then really only for making children. While on the other hand sex means big money and has become one of the most marketable commodities. Pornography has become industrialised to cope with demand caused by the frustration and guilt caused by the moralists. One cannot live without the other. Womens bodies are used to sell products, and sex through prostitution can be bought and sold on the market. The sex market mainly caters for men; womens second class status in society means that they can end up providing some form of sexual service in order to survive. Womens social worth is somehow supposed to be linked to their sexual attractiveness; this constant pressure to be 'beautiful' is making many women's lives a total misery, for some it is literally killing them e.g. anorexia and other dieting disorders.

● Gay Sexuality

The same people who bring us sexism and racism tell us relations between people of the same sex are supposed to be 'wrong', 'evil', and 'unnatural'. The result is frustration and an underground existence for many of us.

Homosexuality, whether lesbian, gay or bisexual is neither wrong or immoral. Its a natural choice for millions of people, a happy and equal one only tainted by the bigotry of others. If sexually mature people choose to love or have sex with each other, that's no one's business but their own, regardless of race or gender.

Anti-gay and lesbian propaganda has been thrust at us, especially in this century, by the ruling and middle classes with their newspapers and TV stations in exactly the same way as racism has. In both cases the objective is the same, to get us to swallow ridiculous stereotypes and divert our anger into attacking those who we have no logical reason to attack. These stereotypes are paper thin and are destroyed every day: there are gay truck drivers and oil-riggers, lesbian nurses and news readers.

No one, apart from those who want us divided, benefits from this homophobia (fear of lesbians and gays). Currently the gay movement is less and less a ghetto and more people are 'coming out' (openly admitting their sexuality). A lot of this is due to the hard work of working class gays and lesbians who have not only had to contend with bigotry but also with middle class power-seekers and reactionaries within their own movements. *WE'RE OUT AND STAYING OUT!*

● Fascism

This is an extreme form of capitalism. It is really a kind of 'super-patriotism' to the nation-state. In practice this means that a so-called national identity is promoted in the working class. This 'national identity' really consists of a more intense form of what the ruling class want us to be normally; racism, sexism, religious bigotry, respect and worship for our 'leaders' and war are all used to pull our class close to the ruling class and their nation-state. It aims to get the working class to identify strongly with the State and the interests of the ruling class in order to oppress them more effectively and destroy opposition from within the class. Fascism is used as an insurance against the threat of a united working class. The various fascist groups and movements are

maintained and tolerated by the ruling class for this purpose. But it is also unstable as it brings maniacs into power e.g. Hitler, and is kept as a weapon of last resort by the ruling class.

Fascism is another way of running capitalism and protecting it. It's not very efficient but is crude and effective and very bad news for our class. Racism is often a strong element in fascism and is used to bind the working class more strongly to the local ruling class e.g. the UK and France. It goes without saying that fascism must be beaten down at every opportunity by our class.

● Poverty of the Spirit

It has to be said that material poverty is not the only kind that our class must contend with.

Earlier in this chapter we discussed the false divisions that are created in the working class; nationalism, religion, sexism, racism, hatred of gays and nationalism. The world we live in is dominated by the ideas and values of the ruling class and these are pushed at us very hard. In their view of the world it is good to be the bully, the snob, the scab, the racist, the anti-gay bigot etc. This has a terrible effect on our personal lives and our communities. They are wrecked by the divisions of fear, mistrust, ignorance and hatred that these ideas bring with them. This reaches every part of our class, both those doing well in secure well-paid jobs and those with next-to-nothing at the bottom of the pile.

In some of our communities the main hobbies are wife-battering, drunkenness, hard drugs, racism, bigotry, robbing off each other and grassing each other up to the cops or the DSS. We have no illusions about the conditions our class live in. The ruling class wants us to hide behind our front doors afraid of each other believing only what we see in their newspapers and TV, living a life of isolation and mistrust. This is the State they try to keep us in to stop us uniting against them. We might not be starving but we are dying of boredom, anger, frustration, stress and ignorance.

It is not surprising that some of us 'go under'; give up hope, lose self-respect, turn to drugs and booze or religion or even fascism. This kind of poverty is different but just as bad as a lack of money. Put the two kinds of poverty together and you have got bad news.

We must now look at how these ideas and divisions are created and kept alive in our class.

How the Political Divisions are Created and Maintained

It becomes quite clear that these political divisions benefit no-one but the ruling and middle classes of our society. But the questions we have to ask ourselves are: how do they get away with it? How is it sustainable over such a long period of time that it becomes a way of life and is accepted as normal? Why is this necessary for capitalism to survive? To answer these questions we must first look at the nature of class domination itself. It is difficult for any ruling class to maintain its rule by force alone, i.e. a straight forward dictatorship. This is inefficient and not likely to succeed in the long run. The ruling class need a minimum amount of co-operation and support from the working class to make the system work, in other words they require a certain amount of consent.

But for people to give their consent to this they have to see things in the same way as their rulers - they must have a common point of view. The ruling class obviously want the working class to see things their way because the easiest way of exercising power is through consent. This point of view is made up of a set of ideas, beliefs and values which represent a particular way of viewing the world, this 'package' is what we call an ideology. There are other ideologies some of which are anti-capitalist.

The ideology of the ruling class is not rigid. To survive it must be flexible, practical and able to respond quickly to the needs of the ruling class in their class struggle with the working class. At certain times this ideology may be brutal and reactionary, and at other times it is more reconciling and reformist. In this country during the last forty-five years there have been many changes in ruling class ideology - from the New Deal under Labour in the 1940's, the consensus welfare politics of the 1950's and 60's, the austerity measures of the 1970's, right through to the 'popular capitalism' of the Thatcherite era of the 1980's. What next for the 1990's and the 21st century?

Mass Culture

Having a coherent ideology is of no use to the ruling class unless it is sold to the working class at every opportunity. This is one of the roles of mass culture. The other role of mass culture is to stimulate mass consumption, i.e. consumerism, in order to create evermore markets to make a profit in. Mass culture also partly fulfils the leisure needs of the working class. The capitalists know that leisure is important to people. Who works just to survive? They also know that 'leisure' is a large market in it's own right.

Mass culture is brought to us through the mass media; books, newspapers, magazines, films, TV, 'pop' music, etc. It does not just sell us products and push political ideas (propaganda), it maintains by subtle ways all the necessary prejudices, myths and stereotypes that keep us ignorant of each other, so fostering fear, isolation and divisions between each other. It is the same old story of divide and rule that keeps us in our place (the bottom) and them in theirs (the top).

A vast industry now surrounds mass culture, including advertising, market research, psychologists, education (especially higher education that researches and experiments with new ideas and methods), public relations firms etc. It is a 'booming' market worth billions to the capitalists. This all reflects the importance and size of the market that is represented by leisure and information in our society, and the need to maintain social stability. Mass culture employs large numbers of middle class people and as we mention elsewhere this is one of the roles of that class in capitalism, and a source of much tension for them

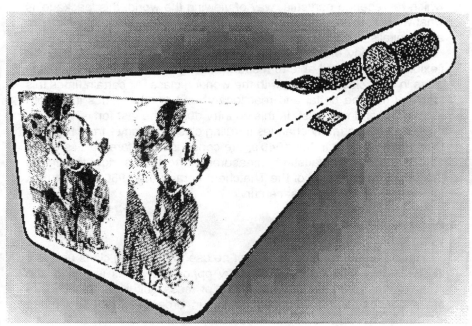

too! As a class they are constantly having to change their view of the world as the needs of their capitalist masters change.

● Mass Culture and Class Culture

Despite all this our class position in society creates a certain culture all of its own that grows around our common class experience. Daily our class around the world share the experience of exploitation at the point of production and consumption, and domination by the State. These things are not imagined. They are real and a powerful force towards unity. Our culture reflects the boredom, alienation and sterility of a class based society; but it also expresses a healthy amount of hostility, conflict and resistance to capitalism and the State. The working class are aware most of the time that they are in an inferior position, and at moments in our daily lives we fight back and gain a space we can call our own. Mass culture tries to join the working class to the middle and ruling class parts of society but it never succeeds. Instead it just papers over the cracks of class divisions.

● Ideology in our Daily Lives

Thinking about ideology doesn't figure much in our daily lives; but it is our very own personal experiences that are shaped by it, in much the same way as it is shaped by class and the economic system. When we are young we are instructed to believe and do certain things; to fill certain roles and ways of behaving; this process is known as 'socialisation'. We learn about sexual roles and behaviour in our families. Parents are under great social pressure to conform to what is known as "responsible parenting". The family is the basic social unit in capitalism and is under extreme pressure as capitalism lurches from one crisis to the other. Now more than ever parents are under pressure to conform and instill the 'right' values in their children. Throughout the 1980's the breakdown of the family was being blamed as the source of social disorder by the politicians. The fact is, the family cannot cope with what is expected of it by capitalism and that is why it is breaking down.

At school this process is carried even further. We learn to obey the all powerful institution of the school and are conditioned to place trust in 'official knowledge'. When we are in our adult lives we are influenced by what is called 'common sense'. This so-called 'common sense' is usually set by the media and politicians. Thus ideology tries to penetrate our very ideas and sense of what knowledge is.

● Conclusions on Ideology and Culture

As was mentioned above both ideology and mass culture are not as all-powerful as they seem. Within our class culture there are the essential elements for class struggle, the ruling and middle class know this only too well. Ideology cannot guarantee 100% allegiance from even the most right-wing of our class. Its main function is to thwart any development of a radical working class consciousness and to seek out discontent and neutralise it. From our point of view it is essential to promote and strengthen the working class culture that already exists. This culture needs to counter the ruling class ideologies such as sexism, nationalism etc. whilst setting its own agenda in the class struggle; making demands that the ruling class cannot even contemplate, let alone fulfil.

● THE WORKING CLASS - ECONOMIC DIVISIONS

Here are some statistics - on the subject of wealth. For this purpose we shall use the measure of "Disposable Income of a Household", as used by the Central Statistical Office (CSO) and others. What this means is the amount of money that a family has left to spend after tax, national insurance, rent or mortgage etc. are paid.

First we took the amount of social security payable to a family unit as the reference point for material poverty in the UK and then set about using the poverty trap tables of gross income versus disposable income found in "Social Trends" from the CSO as a tool. We then applied this tool to the results of the Dept. of Environment Family Expenditure Survey.

This had a sample of 7,081 households, and is carried out regularly. The figures are from 1985. We found that the following number of different households were on and below this arbitrary poverty line (which we think is far too low anyway). Percentages are expressed of the total of that sort of family in the sample; ('Family' in this survey means married man and woman with or without children.)

Families on the poverty line - total percentages;
●*Out of all families with no children 29% are on the poverty line.*

● *Out of all families with one child 20% are on the poverty line.*
● *Out of all families with two dependant children 15% are on the poverty line.*
● *Out of all families with three children 33% are on the poverty line.*

There are large numbers of families only just above the poverty line as well. And the picture gets worse for the old, 75% of all pensioners are on the poverty line. The accuracy of these figures depends on the sample being representative of the general population. Assuming this is so (this type of survey has been going on for years) then the figures make sobering reading. These figures were backed up in late 1990 by a United Nations survey into child health in the UK. The results showed that 25% of British children were malnourished to the extent that their growth was stunted.

Further support is given to our rough figures by an examination of the work of a lefty professor Peter Townsend. In 1979 he published a thousand page survey and examination of poverty in the UK. He says;

"By the State's own definition of poverty (the dole etc.), therefore, there were between 15 and 17.5 million in a population of 55.5 million who were in or near poverty."

"Poverty" by Peter Townsend.

In percentage figures this amounts to about 32% of the total UK population living in poverty. The Professor, after 892 pages of statistics, philosophy and case studies came to the following conclusion;

"The chief conclusion of this report is that poverty is more extensive than is generally or officially believed and has to be understood not only as an inevitable feature of severe social inequality (the class system) but also as a particular consequence of actions by the rich to preserve and enhance their wealth and so deny it to others."

"Poverty" by Peter Townsend.

Well done Prof! However his solution is economic reform by government, which the State and Establishment would not allow to happen, as we all know quite well. But poverty is one thing that can't be denied. Even the dreadful bleeding-hearts liberal paper *The Guardian* admits that there is a large number of the poor.

"According to the Governments Central Statistical Office, the bottom half of society own just 7% of the wealth. In the last decade the

THE POVERTY LINE

FAMILIES BELOW THE POVERTY LINE
FAMILIES= married man and woman with or without children in this 1985 survey

No child — 29%
1 child — 20%
2 children — 15%
3+ children — 33%
Pensioners — 75%
UK total — 32%

UK malnourished children 25%
Source UN 1990

Top half of society own 93% of wealth
Bottom half just 7%

Source Central Statistical Office

POVERTY LINE disposable income after taxes, rent/mortgage etc is paid equivilent to social security level: ie **very low**

gap between the richest and the poorest in our society has widened."
Nigel Fountain - *The Guardian* 30/11/90.

Briefly, we would say that one third of our class live in poverty. Another third earn up to about twice the income of the official poverty line and the final third of our class do better than this. Through the 1980's our class has been squeezed harder with cutbacks in benefits and welfare. So what we have is an economically divided working class as well as all the political divisions that are created to keep us apart.

● Comments on Class - the 'Alternative' Middle Class?

Put brutally, an economically poor offspring of a middle class family still has more power than an average working class person. This power includes; knowing how to 'work the system', a social network that can provide access to money or work, an accent that commands respect from those in authority; the values, attitudes, self confidence and assertiveness that goes with a middle class upbringing. In short a ragged-arsed bare foot hippy from the middle class on the dole is still middle class.

● The Police

The police and similar groups like bailiffs, prison officers and DSS snoopers have a unique role to play in the preservation of the status-quo. Some actually do believe in trying to do good like stopping crime, but such naivety quickly disappears after entering the force. The Establishment only want those people who are suited by character, temperament and politics to join the ranks of the police force. Those unsuited quickly leave. History is full of instances of soldiers etc. coming over to the side of the people in revolutions. The same cannot be said of the police. While most of the police start off from a working class background they cannot be included in our view of the working class. A very large section of our class has a healthy contempt and disdain for this type of traitor and practically keep them at arms length.

● Privileged Working Class? (money but no power)

There always is a section of our class that does better than the rest; remember divide and rule. In recent history we have seen the so-called 'aristocracy' of labour doing very well with workers like printers, car workers, plasterers and some technical workers often earning more than some middle class jobs like teachers, middle management or social workers. This, we are told, heralds the end of the class system, nonsense! Remember it's power that counts.

Printers and plasterers do not have the power of a teacher who has a class of thirty or more people to mould into 'good' citizens or a doctor who has to decide who lives or dies in our inadequate health system, or a social worker who has to decide whether to take your children from you. Power is the deciding factor here. The privileged working class might have a bit of money, a flash car, a house and often a head full of junk! But what they do not have is power or the prestige that goes with it in the British class system.

● Romanticising Poverty

Amongst the Left, especially those from the middle and upper class, there is tendency to be romantic about poverty. Some of the intellectuals see working class people as the "Noble Savage". This is often expressed in their films and books etc. about us. The Russian anarchist Bakunin, who was from an aristocratic background and very sound on most political matters, went so far as to describe tramps as the 'flower of the proletariat'!

We think these attitudes are a hindrance and reflect a middle class obsession which in recent years has resulted in some of the children of the middle class in the UK going off to the inner cities and adopting a 'tramp' drop-out type lifestyle. This strange behaviour is usually accompanied by the use of hard drugs and right-wing individualism hiding behind the label of 'anarchism', which is of course a complete opposite to what anarchism stands for.

This is the latest development in a long line of the bohemian tradition of the middle class. It speaks volumes about the inner misery and despair of middle class life but does little to shed light on life at the bottom of the class system. People from our class tend to see poverty, ignorance and squalor differently. This is how one working class revolutionary saw it,

"A lot of nonsense has been written by sections of the socialist movement about this: to romanticise that way of life is daft. When human beings don't care about their own health or personal cleanliness and think of nothing but drink, they are no good to the movement or to anybody else."

Harry McShane - from "No Mean Fighter", with Joan Smith.

● Internal Differences

Each class has internal differences, grades and prestige. For instance the working class has at the top, the 'privileged' workers (that may aspire to a middle class lifestyle), skilled workers, down through semi-skilled, labourers, and at the bottom the unemployed, etc.

Even the ruling class has grades. For instance the aristocracy are at the top, followed by merchant bankers and established 'old' City of London firms, who look down on stockbrokers and dealers who are regarded as the 'workers' of the ruling class!

These grades and aspirations are useful at keeping people divided. The mere image of the car or house you own is enough to place you in the class system. This is the social function of snobbery, to keep us divided.

● Mobility

The class system is alive and kicking! It is a dynamic set of social relations with people on the way up and on the way down. It is real and the mental hospitals and graveyards are full of its victims. Class politics can be a dangerous game. It is very important to know who you are, where you came from and where you are now in the class system. If you don't, great confusion and stress can result from being involved in active class politics. The middle class are largely recruited from the working class; they do not spring out of the ground! This recruitment has grown largely after World War Two when capitalism expanded so rapidly that it outstripped the supply of middle class people available.

There are of course long established middle class families especially at the upper end of the middle class where they blend into the lower ruling class. Some ruling class people even start out in the working class. The class system in the UK is comparatively static compared to the USA where upward mobility is more open to those with ability and ruthlessness, often called 'meritocracy' by academics. The eleven year reign of Thatcher as UK Prime Minister represented a serious attempt to change Britain towards the American way of doing things. This in itself is a symbol of the struggle going on within the UK ruling class between 'new money' and 'old money'.

There are national differences in class systems but the essentials remain the same everywhere.

● Grey Areas

There are groups of people who appear hard to fit into the class system e.g. artists, dropouts, the self-employed, shopkeepers, students etc. But many of these 'grey areas' only exist in peoples minds through confusion and ignorance, a state of affairs that is essential for capitalism and its class system to survive. The media and education set out to minimise the existence of the class system and stress that everyone is an 'individual' and responsible for how successful, or not, they are. This process blurs the reality of class society and promotes the myth of meritocracy. Concerning artists, they are a good example of the class process at work. Of course there are painters, poets, musicians etc. in the working class, but if they are to succeed in their 'art' and make a living from it then they are under great pressure to enter the middle class, ask them!

Of course everyone is an individual and is also a member of a particular social class. And yes some people are genuinely hard to fit into a class structure, there are always those who do not fit neatly into the scheme of things. That's the genius of humans!

But once you become conscious of the existence of class and start looking at society from a class point of view then the obvious starts to make itself clear. Thus a family can have a son who has joined the middle class and a daughter who is working class. Where before this might have seemed confusing or an 'act of God' or 'fate' it becomes a lot easier to understand. Then you wonder how you ever managed without "class consciousness"! And the grey areas start to shrink.

● Subjective Class

What we have been talking about so far is reality. What we must now look at is what people think about class, i.e. the ideas that have been put in their heads about class. A lot of people think they are in a certain class when in fact they are not. This is "subjective class" and is a result of the propaganda campaign waged against the working class and to a lesser extent against the middle class, to deny and warp peoples' class identity. This campaign plays on our aspirations. Who wants to be a worker at the bottom of the pile? Before we examine subjective class we should state that there are people who are perfectly clear about what class they belong to. The ruling class have a clear understanding of this as do some of the working class and middle class.

● Some Examples of Subjective Class

A working class person might consider themselves middle class because; they own their own house, are self employed or even because they have a nice carpet in their living room! This is what is called wishful thinking. A middle class person might think that they are working class because their parents were working class or because they have chosen to do a manual job as part of a rebellion against their background. As a rule of thumb it takes one or two generations to slide down the class scale from middle class origins. This is because many of the benefits of being middle class are passed on through 'culture' in the form of accent, confidence, education, attitude, ideas, values etc. Funnily enough some middle class people would rather not be what they are, just like some working class people. Its mad really, but that is the stupidity of the class system. In both cases it is wishful thinking.

● SUMMING UP ON CLASS

● There definitely is such a thing as class and the class system will continue to exist as long as there is capitalism, wage labour and governments. Superficial things may change, such as home ownership and holidays abroad for some of the working class in the UK. Class society is a violent, miserable way of organising a society.

● There are broadly speaking three classes; ruling class, middle class and working class. The ruling class have to fight each other and stay on top of everybody else. The middle class can produce competitors for political power with the ruling class and they work very hard to keep society running smoothly by keeping the working class under control. The working class fights back spasmodically against the other two classes sometimes on a massive scale. The rest of the time the working classes fight each other.

● In identifying who is who in the class system, wealth and power are the key factors.

● In order to make a new world without class divisions and the misery that they create for everyone we must first destroy the old world and its class system.

● During a revolutionary period the middle class will split and part of it will side with the revolutionary sections of the working class. Equally, the working class will split between those who support the revolution and those who side with the bosses.

● The ruling class does not secretly conspire to oppress us, most of the time they don't need to. They actually believe their own propaganda. As a class they operate by internal consent, mostly in the open. They are of course also capable of plotting and planning ahead with the aid of the middle class and when the need arises, will use every dirty trick in the book.

● And finally the ruling class rule but does not actually govern. That is left to the State's managers, the politicians and civil service, on a day to day basis.

"There are many thousands of us soldiers who have ventured our lives, who have little property in this kingdom. But it seems now that unless a man has property he has not rights."

"Sir, I see that it is impossible to have liberty but all property must be taken away. It must be so."

The Levellers - *from the Putney debate with Cromwell, 17th century.*

"The Levelution has begun,
So I'll go home and get my gun,
And shoot the Duke of Wellington."

A 19th century street song *from "The Making of the English Working Class", - E.P. Thompson.*

Section Headings
- Introduction.
- Why Working Class Fightback?
- Class Struggle in the UK After 1945.
- The Present and the Future.

● INTRODUCTION

In this chapter it is the struggle of the working class against the rest of 'society' that we are interested in.

● WHY WORKING CLASS FIGHTBACK?

The first question is why? Why do we bother? The answer must be that we find this kind of society lacking and that we cannot get what we want in this world. And for many of us to have any self-esteem in this sick society we have to feel we are fighting back in some way.

At times we have no choice anyway but to fightback. When the ruling class decide to attack us because of an economic crisis and our backs are against the wall many of us decide to have a go. This is where the role of the British Left is crucial to the ruling class. As long as they can divert us into stupid campaigns like getting Labour elected, the ruling class are safe.

● What Do We Want

Housing of the kind we want with enough space to have some peace to ourselves if we want it, enough good food and drink, worthwhile work, a world that is not polluted, the healthcare we need and want, the time to do 'our own thing', education that is not brainwashing, leisure and freedom to enjoy ourselves as we see fit without taking away other individual's freedom in the process. In short, to be free and live in solidarity and peace with each other. This is worth fighting for.

Most of us don't have these things and only a few of us can have some of these things if we work hard, behave ourselves or are very lucky, like winning the pools! It follows that capitalism always exists in a fairly precarious state because the desires of the working class will always be in direct conflict with those of the ruling class. Capitalism's 'accounts books' are constantly having to be balanced by wars, famine, depression, unemployment, etc. Those that maintain capitalism; capitalists, industrialists, financiers, governments, bureaucrats, managers and economists, etc. spend their days working out where they can rip off sectors of society with the minimum of social unrest.

● Bad Dreams for the Ruling Class

In an advanced capitalist country like the UK, the ruling class will try to avoid the use of armed force if at all possible, because once they have done so the delicate 'balance' of their society will be broken and people will start to take sides. An advanced capitalist economy cannot function if a significant part of the working class do not identify with their ruler's values anymore (Northern Ireland is running at a loss). France in 1968 and in the late 1960's the radical black movement in the USA, are good examples of this, and they were only starting to be a threat before they were crushed. This is the nightmare lurking around the corner that 'our' ruling class face in the UK.

To avoid this they use economic force, political isolation and the police against rebellious groups like strikers and the unemployed. For this to work they have to persuade the working class that they have something in common with their rulers. Nationalism, religion, racism, history, education and most recently ecology are being used against us. Crucial to tying all this together is encouraging a respect for the legal framework of the State.

● CLASS STRUGGLE IN THE UK AFTER 1945

It's a two-way street here in the UK. We have seen many ups and downs in the class war between the working class and their enemies.

After World War Two the deal that was reached by the leaders of the labour movement with the rest of the ruling class enabled the working class to rapidly advance their living standards. A national health service, education and housing all resulted from this period. This was possible because the expansion and reconstruction after the war caused an international boom that the UK benefited from as one of the victors of the war. The empire that Britain still possessed after the war acted as a captive market and added to the boom in the British economy. This situation led to a drastic shortage of labour that resulted in the British capitalist class bringing in migrant workers from the Caribbean, Ireland, Asia and elsewhere.

This situation strengthened the hand of the working class and their labour movement representatives who entered the ruling class on the basis of their control of the working class. The UK working class advanced a great deal economically in this period but politically they went into reverse. This period was the high point of the labour movements incorporation into the ruling class. They acted as the left hand of capitalism and the ruling class in this period. But even under capitalism nothing lasts forever and by the early 1970's the boom was coming to an end as international capitalism adjusted its workings to meet the crisis.

The 1979 General Election and the Thatcher years marked the end of the influence of the labour movement in the ruling class. The crisis British capitalism had got into needed a much more radical treatment than the labour movement could deliver. Hence Thatcher. The union leaders were not invited to Downing Street for chats over beer and sandwiches to figure out the best way of shafting the working class.

Instead they were out on their arses! Since then the labour movement has got its act together and is now effectively the left-wing of the Tory party.

● Class Struggle in the UK Since the 1960's

In Britain as in other similar countries the boom was largely built on a surge of manufacturing for the home market and other countries expanding their economies after the war. By the end of the 1960's our captive empire that fuelled the boom was largely gone, and our manufacturing industries had started to transfer to Second and Third World countries where the labour costs were cheaper. This was accompanied by an increase in the finance industry in areas such as banking and insurance and also in specialised hi-tech manufacturing, especially armaments. It is these changes that are at the heart of the social changes and conflicts in Britain during the 1970's and 80's.

● Them

The 1970's saw both the Labour and Tory governments attacking

our social services with cuts in healthcare, unemployment benefit and housing. Cuts in wages, also known as inflation, were rife as was industrial unrest. At one point inflation was running at nearly 30%.

Racism and fascism were sponsored by the Establishment as an attempt to divert working class anger away from the ruling class and their policies to the migrant workers who settled here during the post-war boom. The idea was simply to whip up the sleeping racism of the British working class and 'blame' the blacks and the Asians for unemployment. It nearly worked, the National Front were getting thousands of votes at by-elections.

There followed the election in 1979 of a right-wing government that carried on and intensified the attacks begun by earlier Labour and Tory governments. The methods used had been well thought out. Here's an example - the intense publicity and propaganda campaigns with dirty tricks aimed at discrediting socialist ideas in the working class, many of the techniques refined in the war in Northern Ireland were used, e.g. Pys-ops; psychological warfare aimed at us with lots of scare stories in the press about 'looney lefties', etc. the use of 'black', 'grey' and 'white' propaganda; spies, agent provocateurs, sabotage, blackmail and disinformation about prominent left-wing personalities.

The industrial campaign was carried out by following the infamous "Ridley Plan", named after Sir Nicholas Ridley one of its chief architects. Against the backdrop of the dirty tricks of the mid 1970's they came up with a strategic plan to destroy the power of the unions in the workplace. Secondary to this main assault was a campaign against the Labour Party in local and national government carried out through the media. The industrial plan consisted of deliberately precipitating strikes in chosen industries and defeating each workforce one by one. The 1980's were to be a decade of class war with our side getting a hammering. A right-wing journalist expressed well the attitude of the ruling class.

"Old fashioned Tories say that there isn't a class war. New Tories make no bones about it: we are class warriors and we expect to be victorious."

- Peregrine Worsthorne.

The plan was to pick off individual unions and industries one by one, leaving the hardest, the coal miners, until the last when they would be on their own. It worked. This was helped by the fact that unions were organised by trade and industry and would not come to each others help, a fact that the plan took account of.

The social part of the plan was more exotic, central to it was a series of attacks on the Labour Party. Ridley, Keith Joseph, and other Establishment figures had realised that the Labour Party activists were mainly out of touch with the working class and followed a pretty abstract and elitist political strategy. This was used to portray the Party as being full of 'loony lefties'. More importantly this was used to weaken the hold of basic socialist ideas in the working class such as solidarity, by ridiculing those who claimed guardianship of these ideas. This worked. Alongside this the ruling class encouraged a resurgence of right-wing and fascist movements. This did not just 'happen'. The rise of the National Front was the most visible aspect of this with its considerable success at local elections. Various ruling class individuals and groups were involved in links with European and world right-wing and fascist groups. Another element in the 'social plan' was what we call 'social engineering'. This had two main strategies. Firstly to create a large pool of poor, unemployed people with which to terrify the rest of the working class. Second, to involve the rest of the working class as much as possible in the workings of capitalism. Obviously the aim was to divide the working class enough to prevent us attacking the ruling class.

Mass unemployment (caused by restructuring) for which we were blamed and removal of social security benefits created a pool of poor and desperate people that is still growing today. The deliberate creation of a housing shortage by stopping the council housing building programme was to have a profound effect on our class, and of course resulted in a dramatic rise in house prices. To the rest of us was offered the carrot of buying a council house, going self-employed or getting involved in the service industries. A short economic boom based on credit, (much of it secured against inflated house prices), was used to give credibility to the 'mini-capitalist' dream. The aim was (and is) to mould a generation to right-wing ideas. It is fair enough to say that the ruling class started preparing, in this form, for the coming civil war in Britain at least as early as 1974.

This brings us to the present. We face further attacks but at least the decks are clear for a face to face conflict between our class and the ruling class. The Labour Party and the union leaders have finally identified themselves with the bosses, and the British Left are collapsing, or disowning the working class and denying our existence.

Now it is us and them, with nothing in between.

● Us - Our Hall of Fame!

The 1970's saw many anti-racist and anti-fascist actions carried out with many bitter fights and working class involvement. The industrial unrest of the 1970's culminated in the "winter of discontent" that practically crippled the nation. The early 1970's saw mass power black-outs and the public humiliation of the Tory Heath government by a wave of industrial action. The 1980's too, saw many strikes and amidst the defeat of 'traditional' union methods were some particularly heartening developments. Instead of strikers remaining on the defensive in the face of; new union legislation, military style police, and media lies, they went on the offensive. Their attacks on employers and the police met with considerable success. The imagination displayed was particularly impressive. Of course the labour movement leaders were appalled at this display of working class courage and initiative and condemned these 'criminal elements'.

In our communities the traditional dislike of the police was replaced with a fierce hatred and resistance to arrests that developed into pre-planned attacks. Now every city has at least one 'no-go' area where the rule of law is only partly maintained. In these areas there is an awful lot to be done politically to improve solidarity and awareness in our class but there has been encouraging developments in places like Salford in Manchester, and some communities affected by strikes such as those of the miners, printers and healthworkers. Particularly encouraging in the 1980's were the re-emergence of 'sympathy strikes', such as the actions of Ford car workers, Kent miners and others in support of the Healthworkers disputes.

Our communities have also seen a whole new series of violent riots against the police starting in 1980 in Bristol and continuing up to the present, which themselves are part of a much older tradition. The 'no-go' areas that were defining themselves in these earlier riots were often the poorest and the most pressurised of the working class. Many but not all, were black working class areas, yet white youth travelled miles to join in the fun, a fine example of solidarity in action! It is this fear of provoking all out resistance by a large portion of the working class that guides government and capitalist plans for this country. For instance the miners strike stretched them to the limit. The Tories virtually stated that publicly. It is fairly well known that troops were put in police uniform for picket duty, (miners often met their sons on different sides of the picket lines!) MI5 could not handle the load and

army security was pressed into service. They had plenty of experience of dealing with a hostile civilian population from Northern Ireland.

The British working class is angry and pissed off. They have seen their post-war gains taken away and a drop in their standards of living. They are also as split as ever between those who are 'doing well' and full of patriotic pride and those who feel nothing in common with the system. Our class is boiling with hatred and frustration. Our task is to help direct this anger and energy in the right direction. The situation is very volatile and that is why the present government is treading carefully. Nevertheless our class does not inevitably take the revolutionary option. They can jump the other way into the arms of fascism, this is the final 'insurance policy' for the ruling class and is maintained in the UK, Europe and elsewhere for that purpose.

● THE PRESENT AND THE FUTURE

"I don't pretend to be a prophet, but know this, and lots of my mates know too, that we're not treated as we ought to be, and a great philosopher says to get knowledge is to know we're ignorant. But we've just begun to find that out, and you masters and owners may

look out, for you're not going to get so much your own way, we're going to have some of ours now..."

Anonymous letter from Geordie miner to mine owner - 1831.

We feel that for our class to move forwards we need; pride, identity, solidarity, a sense of history etc. Obviously we see the function of organisations like the Class War Federation as encouraging the taking up of such ideas and attitudes in our class. These have to be defined and spread, especially in the face of opposition from the ruling class, the media, police, Labour Party, unions etc. This will present new challenges. Assuming some of our class are successful in maintaining and advancing a real culture of resistance and solidarity that picks up on older traditions, then they are going to come into conflict with the interests of the ruling class. At this point they will have to overcome a tough set of problems. We think our approach will have an advantage here because the organisations we want to create see their main role to make the working class conscious and self managing. This is what is required for our class to advance its struggle and is far more efficient than all the 'vanguard' parties of Lenin and Co. put together.

● Winding Things Up

At the moment there are two parts of our life that are kept artificially divided; work (or the lack of it) and the community (or lack of it). At the moment one has little to do with the other and this split really represents the way control of our society is divided up between capitalism (work) and the State (community). We would say that we want to remove the divide between life at work and life at 'home', and decide what we do with our lives ourselves.

● At Work

We are caught between the bosses, the unions, and the Left parties. We will probably by-pass them altogether. The London Underground strikes, oil workers actions and the miners and printers hit-squads give an indication of possible future tactics. We realise for practical reasons that such tactics and groups tend to appear suddenly to do their job and then disappear, often leaving the unions, semi-official groups and opportunists to tidy up the loose ends. We anticipate more similar independent actions in the workplace. The question is how could such groups and movements communicate with each other and help each other? What we imagine is the forming of 'networks' of people and groups in industry, who besides being active in industrial organisation against employers are also 'political', and blend the two together. Politics as opposed to just economic demands would be necessary for such networks to survive the reformists pressures of the outer defences of capitalism i.e. the unions, Labour Party and Left parties. Of course the increasingly aggressive manager class and the cops would be immediate problems as well!

These different network groups would have to get the resources to produce propaganda and pay for practical work. There would be differences in their approach and politics. The need for tactical unity is obvious but we envisage a lot of debate and change at this point, as is usual when working class people are involved in struggles. On past experience in such situations one of the main occupations is 'talking politics' this tends to have a snowball effect on awareness. In these situations mutual education can become a reality. There would definitely be a need to break down the divisions between different sections of industry as at present maintained by the trade union system. The split between work and the community would also have to be broken down. The miner's and printer's support groups were a step in this direction. The geographical separation between work and where we live is a growing factor and will present some problems.

● In the Community

The social engineering and push to fragmentation in our communities by the ruling class would have to be countered. To do this it would need to be identified as such. This would form a continuing part of our theoretical work. Basic work on identity and solidarity needs to be done using local issues such as housing, policing, crime, hard drugs, the environment etc. Separate communities would need to reach out to others in the area and in the region for support and resources. The use of existing organisations might be possible; football teams, clubs, pubs, schools, workplaces etc. The local culture and pride should be utilised. Local history is always popular, folk and music traditions where they still exist; and rebuilding them where they are weak. Media attention grabbing celebrations and commemorations of past local events e.g. the destruction of Bristol Jail, the burning down of Luton Town Hall (1919), the Peterloo Massacre, the Invergordon and Spithead naval mutinies, the Glasgow George Square riot, the Highland Clearances etc. Erecting plaques (even temporary ones) to such local working class heroes and heroines and their actions e.g. Trafalgar Square 1990, could be excellent publicity exercises and be very useful at retrieving our history. These types of methods have all been used successfully elsewhere (Ireland, Europe, South America etc.). We can't see why they would not work here.

The growth of independent community groups in different areas with different emphasis is highly likely e.g., 'families against smack', womens groups, black groups, prisoners and their support groups etc. Encouraging these groups to get in touch with each other would be very valuable for breaking down divisions in our class and building a class struggle based movement which took account of diversity and different origins. To help make this a reality the following list gives a shorthand version of what our class is going to need; identity, pride, solidarity, self management, internationalism and the emergence of a genuine working class culture (also called the 'culture of resistance') that has these things at its centre. This should also form part of the basic objectives of organisations like the Class War Federation.

A very real bonus of this growth of solidarity and defiance will be a big improvement in the quality of life in our communities. What we see happening is the emergence of a real community from the present nonsense of capitalist social relations. A divided and isolated community is weak and petty crime and bigotry are all too common. With a little growth of self confidence and solidarity these problems could be overcome with a very small amount of effort. People who are used to seeing off the police, bailiffs, bosses and other such scum are much less likely to put up with anti-social behaviour from their own kind. This was remarked on by those involved in the miners and printers strikes of the 1980's. Their solutions are likely to be simple and effective.

The following chapter deals with the next phase of destroying capitalism and the State - moving from struggle to the offensive, and on to revolution. We hope to show that in this process of struggle the outlines of the coming new world are beginning to become clear and that a better way of life for us all is far from being a daydream, but is within our grasp now.

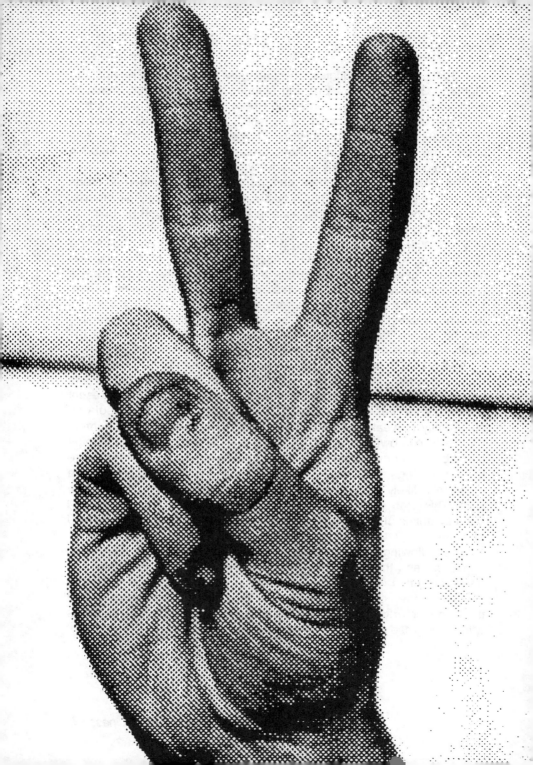

'You must not forget we can also build. It is we the workers who built the cities here in Spain and in America and everywhere. We, the workers can build others to take their place. And better ones! We are not in the least afraid of ruins. We are going to inherit the earth; there is not the slightest doubt about that. The bourgeosie might blast and ruin its own world before it leaves the stage of history. We carry a new world here, in our hearts. That world is growing this minute.'

Buenaventura Durruti - *Spanish revolutionary anarchist, 1936*

Section Headings
- Introduction.
- The Anarchists and the Left.
- The Class War Approach.
- Problems Facing the Revolution.
- The Revolution.
- Summary.

● INTRODUCTION

In this chapter we shall look at how progress can be made from class struggle towards a revolution involving large sections of the working class. We will examine what the working class need, what will be required of us and the likely problems our class will encounter. But before we get stuck in to the nitty-gritty, here's a brief summary of where we are in the class struggle now;

● Struggle is inevitable because society is divided into two opposing camps, the working class and the ruling class, who are fundamentally at odds in this world.

● As things stand now struggles are reformist. The ruling class tolerate unions and opposing parties as a means of diverting the anger of our class into reformism.

● All struggles by the working class have revolutionary potential. That is not to say that every strike or community unrest has the potential to become a revolution. But all struggles that place us in conflict with our enemies have the potential to create self confidence, defend or win gains, change peoples ideas and create revolutionaries, all necessary to turn reform into revolution.

So, how do we see revolutionary ideas successfully replacing reformist ones on a mass scale? Some ideas such as commemorations and independent workplace and community groups have already been touched upon. But before going further we'll take a look at how the Left and anarchists see change occurring and their strategies for encouraging it. We will then describe what we think is required and how class struggle can progress towards revolutionary class struggle.

● THE ANARCHISTS AND THE LEFT

● The Left

The Left parties and groups who espouse revolution have at their

core "the Party". Party leaders analyse the struggle and make statements and/or demands they think appropriate to a particular struggle. The demands they make are usually, but not always, reformist as the idea is to pull as many people as possible behind the demands or statements that the Party makes. In this way they aim to gain mass support for what they are saying and therefore support for their party. Then the Party, with enough support, takes power on the backs of its supporters, become the new rulers and solve all our problems!

Unfortunately this fairy tale ending has never happened although the Left have had plenty of practice around the world. The problems with this approach are as follows:- the initiative and control for the making of reformist and even revolutionary demands and deciding strategy lies in the hands of the Party. The reason for this is the belief in Lenin's words that "the working class can only ever achieve a trade union level of consciousness". Therefore the Party must be there to provide the political, theoretical and organisational leadership for the working class because we are assumed to be to thick to take the lead ourselves. You can see the attraction this must have for the middle class!

This leaves an exclusive elite (the leadership) within the Party asserting their ideas before, during and after the revolution. All we are being asked is to support a different set of bosses. Of course they make out that they will be 'good' bosses, but we will not be able to take back the control of our own lives, except on their terms. There are many different revolutionary Left parties claiming to be the 'correct' party to follow. But their track record is disastrous. They patronise and generally piss off working class people and turn others into cynics - a great waste in our mind. Where such Parties have actually gained power they have been either hopeless or every bit as bad as the capitalists.

● The Anarchists

The anarchists are harder to pin down over their idea of how struggle will turn to revolution. We'll ignore the middle class mutant-dropouts, the 'back to nature' types and the anarcho-fashion rebels that constitute a miserable ghetto of their own. The anarchist movement mainly leans to what is called 'class struggle anarchism'. This is the predominant stream of anarchist thought, the activists involved in this tend to busy themselves as follows. Producing propaganda exposing 'the system' and the nasty individuals within it, getting involved in solidarity work such as with strikes and prisoners particularly, following a hotch-potch agenda of home-grown issues, and organising and communicating through a loosely associated 'anarchist scene'. There are several national class struggle anarchist oriented groups. These work theoretically and organisationally in a federal structure *(see Chapter Seven for a description of federalism)*. They also publish analysis of local, national and international developments. These organisations are useful in combating the slur against anarchism that it is too vague. They have the worthy aim of a total social, economic and political revolution.

The anarchists are good at crying 'wolf' at the world we live in, but hatred or being 'dreamy' are all too often applied to the struggle to gain support for anarchism. They are, in strategy, at the opposite end of the spectrum from the Left parties. They hope that some sort of spontaneous mass uprising and revolution will develop on its own. To reflect this their organisations are loose and political emphasis varies from one anarchist to another, making them confusing and elusive.

To sum up. While the Left tell the working class what to do, the anarchists hope that the working class will one day, all at the same time, realise what to do. Criticism such as this is easy. There are elements from the Left and anarchism that are useful just as there are people doing good work coming from each position. But are we any further on in finding an effective way of turning struggle into revolution?

● THE CLASS WAR APPROACH

Well, the first point to make is that there are no magic formulas, no Five Year Plans. There are though, approaches that combine various political trains of thought and methods of organisation. We would now like to present you with a broad outline of these and then demonstrate the chances of them succeeding by comparing them to developments in recent struggles. We have divided the next section into two parts - practical and theoretical, this is just for our convenience, the two are inseparably linked.

● Practical

As part of the working class we are involved in everyday struggles, we fight to make gains, defend those gains and oppose losses to our freedom and standard of living. This situation begs for a revolutionary and not a reformist perspective. In this respect we see no need to make revolutionary demands on behalf of the working class. But we do see the need to play up the revolutionary elements within these struggles. To enlarge these elements of struggle towards greater self-organisation, solidarity and awareness. The use of humour and imagination in this process helps get these ideas and values in the minds of working class people collectively. The object of this activity is to create a popular 'culture of resistance'. This is the popularisation in the working class of ideas and values that include pride, identity, solidarity, self-management and internationalism.

Fundamentally this is about bringing politics into all areas of peoples lives. As we have seen in earlier chapters the capitalists invade every area of our lives, in turn the working class have to retrieve every part of their lives - the old feminist proverb that the personal is political is true here. This development becomes the foundation and energy behind any possible revolutionary movement. In areas of the world where this has happened, such as Scotland, Spain, Italy, and Russia the traditions have lingered on generations after the original movements were crushed. It's powerful stuff!

In the process of developing this culture of resistance we need to assess the ideas being developed both in our class and by our enemies in the ruling class. For this, complimentary activity is required in addition to the active agitation, confrontation and propaganda that we need to do. This is where 'theory' comes in.

● Theoretical

As the class war between us and the enemy hots up our class will create various forms of activity briefly touched upon in the previous chapter; federations, networks, local groups in the community and workplaces, as well as special interest groups such as prisoners and gay and lesbian groups etc. and independent groups loosely affiliated to the movement - such as propaganda and entertainment groups. This kind of blossoming of activity outside of the central control of the State and the Left parties will be essential to the push towards revolution.

Alongside this development and as a part of it, there must be continuous political debate and mutual education within the working

class. The awakening in struggle that many working class people experience, and remark on, in strikes and riots etc. usually creates a great hunger for knowledge, we keenly feel the need to understand our position in the world as individuals and as a class. It is this exciting process that the Left call developing 'class-consciousness'.

It is essential that a growing number of individuals can inject revolutionary ideas into present struggles and in the same process develop their own ideas personally. This is a two way process. Organisations similar to the Class War Federation can play a crucial role in this respect, as being part of the support network that the revolutionary elements within the working class will need.

We must emphasise here that the job of such organisations is not to detach ourselves from our class like the vanguard parties of the Left, who have a terrible track record in wasting and disillusioning some of the best working class activists they attract. No, our tactic must be the reverse, to move further into the class, so that revolutionary ideas and values such as solidarity, identity, pride etc. start to become a habit. In this way we can, with others, make a more effective impact on the struggle we are involved in.

We understand that to destroy capitalism a movement will have to grow within the working class that is diverse yet coherent in its ideas. In other words people and groups from very different backgrounds and experiences will have to come together and work together; from prisoners to blacks, to gays and lesbians, to workplace groups and womens groups and so on. This diversity of approaches and emphasis is a strength in developing a culture of resistance but the only cement that can hold it together is the power of ideas.

These are not ideas handed down to us on a plate from some marginal group of lefties or intellectuals but ideas developed and worked out together by working class people in everyday life and in everyday struggles. (During this century and the one before the working class has had its own debating clubs, libraries and corresponding clubs).

We have with the rest of our class an economic and social tie but when we stand shoulder to shoulder together on the barricades it should not just be because we are stuck in the same boat; it should be because we have our eyes wide open and are fighting to create a better world for us and our children.

Quite simply, if the revolution we hope for has a chance of happening and surviving it will be because the working classes have the right ideas in their heads for the job.

● Not a Fantasy

This type of growth of a culture of resistance and class consciousness is always a very real possibility, one that the ruling class understand very well. We have only to look at past struggles to see this. The 1984/85 miners strike was notable in a number of ways. Support groups and strike committees were widespread and effective. Food distribution and welfare advice were, amongst other things, self organised in mining communities. The 'hit squads' of the miners (and printers) were direct, courageous and imaginative while the picket lines were full of humour and political debate.

"During that year of struggle and unity many mining women like me discovered our true selves. This new woman revealed a multitude of talents that she developed and used during the strike. We can never go back to being those ordinary housewives tied by tradition to our homes. We have changed, for the better and forever. We look at everything in a different way. We are now active in our communities. We meet regularly to tackle local and national issues that need our

attention.."
Sian James - Chair, South Wales Womens Support Group.

"We no longer regard ourselves as housewives, we are soldiers in the struggle."
Angela John, wife of a striking miner.

Barriers in our class can be quickly broken down in struggle as it becomes obvious who are our friends and who are our enemies. In the 'News International' printing dispute at Wapping in London some of the arrogant Left and hippy anarchists naively scoffed at the print workers because they worked for a company that produced racist, sexist and anti-gay literature. Yet to see those same printworkers warmly applauding and welcoming the lesbian and gay groups supporting them was, to say the least, heartening.

In the anti-poll tax campaign many people attended rallies, held community meetings and organised local and national activities to defeat the hated tax. This was all done in the face of all the usual nonsense from the Left parties who were trying to organise us, recruit us and take the credit for our successes. They were shocked and dismayed when we bypassed them to riot and revolt all around the country and at Trafalgar Square in London.

This is the exciting revolutionary potential of the working class in struggle. To say that this can be built upon in the manner we have described is no idle fantasy.

● THE PROBLEMS FACING THE REVOLUTION

But our class will encounter problems in moving from struggle to revolution and here we are going to discuss some of them.

When we start to become organised and aware on a mass scale the ruling class will pull out all the stops to keep the revolution at bay. We will look at what we can expect from the ruling class in a moment but first we should look at the problems we will face from within the working class.

As we described earlier the strategy of the Left parties is to pull as many people behind them as possible, changing their line as often as necessary. The possibility of a Leninist grouping hi-jacking our struggle must be taken seriously, history shows us all too many examples of just this happening. To combat this we see the need to create independent revolutionaries and groups within the working class. We also see a deep suspicion of the Left parties as being part of the culture of resistance.

There will also be a need to tackle the deeply ingrained right-wing ideas that exist within sections of our class; racism, religion, royalism, nationalism etc. that are at the moment fostered in our class to keep us divided. In a period of intense struggle that looks dangerously revolutionary these same ideas will be used to push sections of the working class towards fascism. At the same time there will be intense anti-communist and anti-anarchist propaganda rubbishing the failed revolutions of the USSR and elsewhere.

The ruling class are reluctant to use the fascists because they are not reliable and can turn on their masters, like Hitler did. Nevertheless, fascism is the insurance policy the ruling class hold against working class rebellion and this is the reason that they support and fund the fascists throughout Europe and elsewhere. Fascism is a problem that our class has to deal with.

Seeing through the false divisions maintained by the ruling class is a crucial activity, its not something that comes secondary to direct confrontational action. It is an essential part of building a culture of resistance and developing a class consciousness where we make an unbreakable bond of solidarity within our class. This is the basis for building a new world, and will be gone into in more detail in the next chapter.

There are also the dangers of things happening without mass support. This is a tricky one. Revolutions can develop very quickly when sections of the working class get fired up. To be successful in actually winning a revolution and creating a new world we must have a reasonable level of solidarity and class consciousness in the working class. International links will be needed to move forwards against capitalism permanently.

This is not to say that we should sit in ivory towers waiting for a mass international, class conscious movement to come knocking on our door! We'd grow old waiting if this was the case. But neither are we prepared to pitch into a suicidal and poorly thought out and poorly supported revolutionary push. Some anarchists see every dispute as a potential route to 'the big one'. We share their optimism, but can not let this get in our way of calmly assessing the potential of this or that struggle. Having said that, if sections of our class rally behind the banners of revolution we'll not be there saying "comrades, wait!". We do have good reason for believing that even from humble beginnings that revolutionary success is a very real possibility.

Besides, the advance towards the revolution is never smooth. Many of our class will find themselves in the position of having to fight back. Often we find ourselves in the position of having to "go with what we've got". James Connoly in Ireland, Zapata in Mexico and Makhno in the Ukraine are good examples of this.

● Internationalism

In earlier chapters we've explained the economic and social similarities that bind us together as a class. Now, internationally, capitalism and its class system touches everyone's lives. Despite our differences in language and culture, we have, undeniably, a link with the working classes of the world.

We are now in a global economy that is in deep trouble. We don't have to stare into a crystal ball to realise what the immediate future holds for our class: a more desperate ruling class launching evermore vicious attacks on us the working class. Building an international revolutionary working class movement is not just a good idea, it is essential.

So far we have looked at gaining support for revolutionary ideas and increasing class consciousness, the need to prevent the Left and the Right from hi-jacking the struggle, the need for sound, clear thinking on our part and internationalism. Now we should look at what we are going to face from the ruling class.

● The Enemy

In earlier chapters we looked at how the ruling class keep on top of society by propaganda, economic power and the brute power of the State both legal and military. On the propaganda front we understand the need to advance our alternative view of society that attacks negative ideas such as racism, sexism, nationalism etc. and the need to stress the positive aspects of current struggles such as solidarity, courage, self-management and imagination.

This work would also seek to undermine ruling class propaganda in as many ways as possible. In this respect the use of humour should not be under-estimated. Every possible media will be used; graffiti,

jokes, stickers, posters, leaflets, newspapers, music and football fanzines, magazines, poetry, song, pirate TV and radio, audio and video cassettes, public meetings, exhibitions, comics and debating clubs etc. As pointed out earlier this kind of activity is the cement that will hold our class together against the attacks of the enemy and their lackeys. We can expect an intense propaganda campaign aimed at the active sections of our class. The example of Northern Ireland has much to teach us about what to expect.

In this connection we can expect the ruling class to try and discredit revolutionary groups and individuals by many means. Simple 'black' propaganda, i.e. lies, is always used, but the skill of the media and security services is in mixing these lies with 'grey' and 'white' propaganda ('grey' is a mixture of truth and lies and 'white' is simple truths). Although the British security services and the media like to give the impression that they are invincible the truth is rather different.

The 'iron-men' of the SAS regularly got bumped off when they were in Aden in the Middle East and now in Northern Ireland. And the recent propaganda campaigns against the miners, printers, rioters, Irish etc. are falling apart with judgements, convictions and rulings being overturned regularly in the courts and large sums of compensation being paid out e.g. for the miners at the 'Battle of Orgreave'. But the miners strike is a good example of the power of the media. By simple techniques such as editing their film so that the miners were shown attacking the police first and then the police shown counter-attacking they gave the impression that the miners were all crazed nutters. The truth was that the police attacked first, as at Orgreave. And the media wonder why people think they are scum who are not to be trusted!

Another favourite method of the State is to carry out some barbaric act, such as bombing a train and blame it on some revolutionary organisation. This also has the added bonus of justifying more repressive action against the working class generally. There are well documented cases of this type of practice in Northern Ireland (e.g. the Miami Show Band killings) and Italy (the Bologna train station bombing). The activities of the secret police in South Africa are very relevant to this as well.

The State is fond of planting spies in movements and groups for obvious reasons. Another tactic is to plant people called agent-provocateurs. Their purpose is to provoke people into some act or other that the State can then use as justification to move against. Planting people in organisations and groups to spoil their internal workings is another method. For obvious reasons these people are called 'spoilers', their favourite method is to create a rift over an organisational or political matter. The Black Panther Party in the USA was an FBI target for this type of action in the 1960's and 70's, as was the radical feminist movement.

There is no sure defence against any of these activities. We have much to learn from those fighting imperialism elsewhere in the world. But life will be difficult for these agents if we succeed in creating a movement that is very diverse and organised from the bottom up with no 'leadership' that can be easily picked off. The very public nature of this movement will also be an obstacle to this kind of attack as spies prosper best in semi-secret organisations.

This does bring us to a very important point. Individuals and groups that do come to some kind of prominence, and they will, are sure to be singled out for attention by the security forces and media. This is fairly inevitable and people should consider carefully the consequences of involving themselves in this kind of public political work. Some individuals will be destroyed by the State, that is certain, again; look at events in Ireland with the Army and RUC death squads.

This is done in order to terrorise the rest of the working class and the activists. But such a loss will not be a body blow to the movement, organisationally or theoretically. If it is, it will be because we have created the wrong kind of movement. We do not mean to sound callous; an injury to one is an injury to all. We know what has to be done and what is likely to happen, there is no point in trying to fool people about this.

● THE REVOLUTION

● On the Brink

The classic sign of gathering revolution is when alternatives to the States power start to co-exist within the same society. Examples would be 'no-go' areas that are also 'no-go' areas for racists, bullies, rapists etc. and leisure activities outside State and commercial control. In the economic sphere this would be accompanied by activities of production and distribution carried out for communal needs and organised communally e.g. health, building, transport, food etc.

Struggles would no longer be about things like rent, housing, policing, dole money, and unemployment they would be about who controls the workplace and the community. At this stage there would start to occur large scale seizure of the means of production (factories, materials, machines etc.) and distribution (offices, communications, lorries etc.). A good example of this seizure of the means of production (also called expropriation) was the 1974 revolution in Portugal where land and factories were taken over.

At this point, and probably long before, our class will certainly come to the position where they face all the armed forces of the State. Previous struggles demonstrate that many of the armed forces will change sides (Portugal 1974, Russia 1917, Ireland 1916-21, China, Cuba etc.) but the secret service, special branch and 'elite' army units would probably remain intact as would some of the airforce - an important weapon. Then there would probably be intervention from NATO and EEC forces hence the need for a truly international revolution. Our class would have to face up to the military aspect of revolution and overcome it. Workers militias and revolutionary armies will have to be considered bearing in mind the dangers of these forces becoming detached from our class and becoming a new power in themselves.

But this problem is not insurmountable. In the Ukraine such armies repelled both the Tzars armies and those of the Bolsheviks. In Spain the same methods were used and were very effective. While in Nicaragua, a tiny country, the working class toppled a dictator and fought off everything short of a full military scale invasion by the USA.

● The Capitalists, Violence and the Revolution

We need to take a serious look at the response of the capitalist class and their servant, the State. They are the masters of physical and mental brutality and revel in it as their privilege of power. We on the other hand suffer the violence of their society every day and have no love of it, but do see violence as necessary and inescapable. Here is a vision of what we are up against;

"The State knows what most lefties ignore, that is that revolution is possible and is a real danger to its existence. It will try to isolate revolutionary elements with the help of the official organisations (unions, communist parties, socialist and labour parties, even most of the left-wing groups). Its strategy will probably consist of separating revolutionary areas from others. Its ultimate tactics will include systematic destruction in these areas, so as to prevent them evolving toward communism by destroying its material conditions: industry, power, transport, etc. It will not hesitate to annihilate these areas if necessary, using the same methods it used in the Second World War (Dresden, Tokyo, Warsaw, Coventry, Hiroshima). Before reaching this stage, it will try to crush the revolutionary movement by using elite troops. If we consider the problem from a simple material point of view, the superiority of capital is remarkable: our only hope lies in a subversion so general and yet coherent that the State will be confronted by us everywhere.

One of the strengths of the capitalists is that people - even the proletariat - just do not imagine how far the State will go in civil war. Many future events will surprise them. It is very useful to point out now the important aspects of the future civil war."

From "The Eclipse and Re-emergence of the Communist Movement" - by Barrot and Martin.

● Democracy and Revolution

A revolution is not 'democratic' in the sense that there might be a majority of our class involved. Although there might be widespread passive support in our class and elsewhere (which is important) those actually participating might be a minority.

As pointed out earlier, many so-called 'anarchists' and 'communists' in the UK seem to believe a revolution is the whole people rising spontaneously like a massive wave and sweeping away the ruling class. Such people would rather avoid the realities of the future in the same way that they seek to avoid those of the present. These people cannot swallow what many in our class already realise. That a revolution means civil war for our class.

● Our Job - What is the Role of the Federation?

Our role in organisations like the Class War Federation should now be pretty clear from what has been said before. Simply, the strategy of our organisation and others like it should be guided by what our class needs to become revolutionary. It should also be obvious, we hope, that the sort of political activity and work that is required of us is best done out in the open. In this way each individual and group comes to

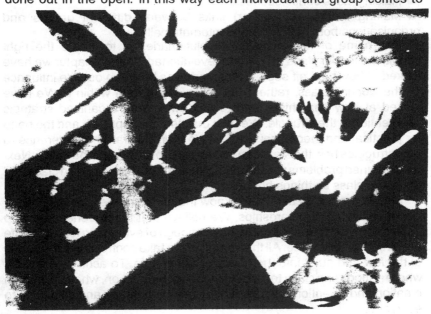

be a representative of the revolution, something that earlier generations of revolutionaries understood well. This kind of work needs clear thinking, determination, humour and some courage.

Those that sneer at such mundane activity and have dreams of the 'armed struggle' or nothing should stay out of our way, or catch a plane to the Palestine or Beirut. The military organisation of the revolution is not our job, nor could it be, for what we see as obvious reasons.

● A SUMMARY

We recognise the problems we face. We have no easy task, particularly as we seek true social, political and economic revolution to form a totally new world. But much of what may be seen as problems and obstacles now to forming a revolutionary movement in the working class would also become our strengths once things started moving; the 'snowball effect' that the ruling class dread. These present obstacles and future strengths are:
● Creating a culture of resistance.
● Advancing practical solidarity.
● Raising class consciousness.
● Making federal (or similar) links between different groups and organisations both nationally and internationally.

The name of the game for revolutionaries is to create the right conditions for our class to become revolutionary. In this chapter we have looked at how the Left see revolutionaries as being an outside influence on the working class, rather than a growing current within it. We have looked at how anarchists tend to shy away from organised strategic intervention in the struggle. We then outlined our approach and the need for practical and theoretical activity. We then illustrated by reference to past struggles how the step from reform to revolution might be made. Next we examined problems we can expect to face both from our own class and the ruling class as things hot up.

So, we are not dreamers, we know the problems we face but believe our goal is worth the hardships. We believe that the material means to enable everybody in this world to have enough of everything for a good life are already in existence. All that remains is to take control out of the hands of the few and put it into the hands of the people. To achieve a society where nobody can claim to own the means of production, where all human creation and invention are part of our common heritage and so belong to everyone.

● A New World?

Now its time to think of brighter and happier times which is after all what we want and what makes us into revolutionaries and class warriors in the first place!

From what we have said so far it should be clear that the foundations of the new world that we hope for are in the process of being laid in present struggles. The next chapter looks at the kind of world that might be built on such foundations.

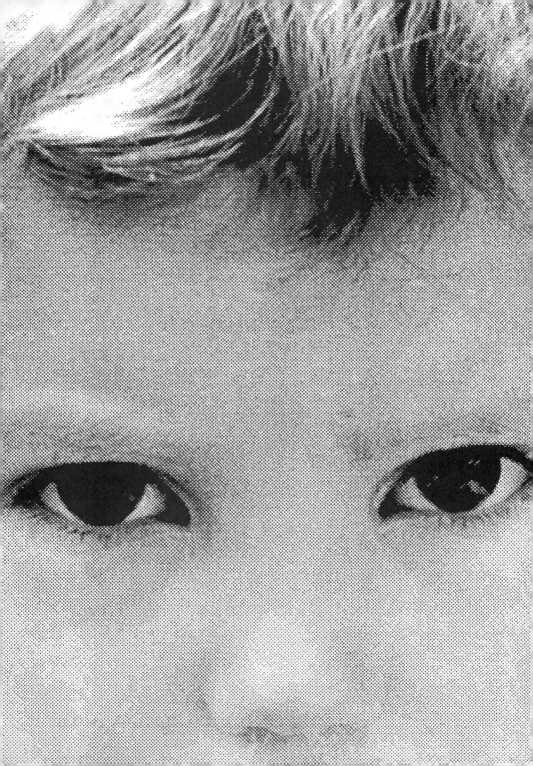

"Its coming yet for all that"
Robert Burns - *Scottish poet.*

Section Headings
- Introduction.
- The Benefits.
- Are We Good Enough?
- Summing Up.
- Conclusion.

● INTRODUCTION

We have examined the unequal, divisive and miserable nature of capitalism, the State and the kind of society that they produce. We have examined ways of building for and achieving a revolution: a genuine revolution involving a complete change about in society.

All the work and hardship required leaves you asking - "Will it all be worth it?" or "What will society be like after a revolution?". Addressing this very point Engels, who worked closely with Marx, said something along the lines of;

"But what will there be new? That will be answered when a new generation has grown up."

"Origins of the Family, Private Property and the State" - F. Engles.

This has been mouthed by many left-wing parties ever since. In fact these parties know exactly how their future society is to be because they aim to be the new bosses in the workers State! We on the other hand think that now is the time to think about what the new world will be like. We make no apologies for rubbing our hands with glee at the prospect of a better way of life. Its time to take a look in general terms at what we are aiming for. First we look at what goes out with the old world and the advantages of leaving it behind and then we look at what the new world will bring in with it and how new attitudes and approaches can be used to deal with old problems.

● THE BENEFITS

Here we look at the benefits we can look forward to in the new world. We will try to give you an idea by looking at three things we see not being present in this new world; artificial divisions, class, money, and the benefits of doing so.

● Artificial Divisions

What goes. Racism, sexism, the hatred of gay and lesbian people etc. As described earlier, during the build upto and in the process of revolution these divisions will be confronted and attacked. We see the new world continuing to smash these false divisions, replacing them with mutual respect, tolerance and understanding. We recognise that many bigoted and reactionary values are deeply ingrained in our class but as we pointed out in Chapter Three on class they are artificially maintained. People can and do change their minds. With the removal of ruling class propaganda we will see a rapid change in society.

Whether you are black or white, female or male, heterosexual or homosexual, makes no difference to your ability to play an equal and active role in the revolution. This point will be hammered home time and time again.

What comes in. There will be no more stereotypes or impossible role models to try and live up to, no more macho posing or female feebleness. No one will be blamed individually or as a social group (e.g. blacks or gays) for the frustrations of others or the problems of society. We will no longer have a pecking order where we compete against each other to find out who is the prettiest, strongest etc.

● Home and Work

What goes. At the present our lives are split between the world of work and that of the community. This will go.

Before and during a revolution we will seize control of our workplaces and communities. We see the groups that will do this as crucial to continuing to provide goods and maintain services. But we also see the need for developing new ways of organising where we live and work *(see the section on class later in this chapter)*. As far as the present artificial divide between work and where we live is concerned, we see work as work wherever it is done. The stupid idea that cooking, washing, gardening, child care etc. are any less work than emptying bins, driving a combine harvester or teaching maths will be buried by us.

What comes in. There will be no need to work for a capitalist to survive. The revolution will mean us clocking-off wage slavery for good! Work will be shared and goods produced and services maintained for the benefit of all. No one will slave hours on end while others are unemployed. Work will no longer be graded into categories judged by status and earning power. Someone keeping a hospital clean will be as important as a surgeon.

● Borders

What goes. We seek to do away with artificial boundaries and borders. The world will not be divided into countries or States by lines drawn on a map by capitalists to mark out their property. We will ignore these borders just as we will tear down the fences and walls surrounding the palaces and estates of the rich.

What comes in. There will be no limitations on travel. There will be no offices or houses stood empty 'out of bounds' to us. All such properties will be used by us, for us. There will be no exclusive banqueting halls or luxurious bosses quarters for the few. We all deserve luxuries in this our only life.

● Class

What goes. There will be no more class system, just people. Instead of the ruling class and middle class dominating our lives we will organise ourselves. There will be no more governments, no more party political broadcasts, no more lying and cheating politicians. There will be no more snobbery and all the petty jealousy that go with it. There will be no more politicians or bureaucrats forcing their laws down our throats.

What comes in. We see a different organisation of society where everybody plays their part in deciding what is going to be done. People will work and live together locally, regionaly and internationally through federalist structures. Federalism is a way of social organising that brings together independent groups that come together for commonly agreed purposes and agree to co-operate with majority decisions. In this set up, each person and group at all levels has the freedom to argue their position and if they choose, to leave the federation altogether.

The ground work for this new way of organising will be laid before and during the revolution, as is indicated in the chapters on Class Struggle and Revolution. The emphasis is going to be on practical self management, the need to respect though not necessarily blindly follow the wishes of the majority. This requires the use of delegates, who are recallable, instantly, to represent our views to other groups and free access to information.

It is important to point out here to cynics that pretty well any structure may be abused by power seekers. An obvious defence against this is by constantly refining and re-examining organisational structures. Although this is very important the best defence against allowing new power groups to form and bring back class divisions is a political awareness and strength in the members of the new society.

● Money

What goes. It is often said that money is the root of all evil. We don't believe this but we do believe that after the revolution we can and will thrive without it. As we approach a revolution it will lose its value as shops, warehouses, farms and factories are taken over and millions start to refuse to pay taxes, bills etc. Money will not be replaced by something with a different name that does the same thing such as bartering, coupons, tokens etc. All forms of exchange value will be opposed. The use of money as a means of valuing things and people is central to capitalism. Profit is stored as capital in the form of money and property which is given a monetary value, *(please refer to the Great Money Trick appendix)*. In this situation all social and economic relations between people come to have a monetary foundation; what Marx called the "cash nexus", the ability and worth of a human being comes to be seen in terms of their property or earning and spending power. Just by its existence, money is a measure of the failure of society to organise the production and distribution of goods for the benefit of all; *IT HAS TO GO!*

What comes in. No bills, taxes, entrance fees, giros, post offices, banks, credit cards, phone cards, meter tokens, debt collectors, insurance premiums, mortgages, rent, wages, national insurance, VAT, pension contributions, bank loans, just for starters!

The above list makes you realise just how much work is done within capitalism in paying, collecting and monitoring money. The present finance sector in countries like the UK employs many people in banking, insurance, unit trusts, foreign currency markets, building societies, pension funds, merchant banking, futures markets, and so on. Every business, government, shop and leisure complex has workers doing hours of totally worthless accounting and paper work. Putting that labour power into something useful and constructive could transform our lives and our world.

● ARE WE GOOD ENOUGH?

We're often told that, "there will always be greedy people who want more than others; that's just the way people are". There are many variations on this theme but we're basically always being told that people are not trustworthy or nice enough to create a better world or live in peace and harmony. In fact governments, the religions and the capitalists they support tell us at every opportunity that we are 'bad' and cannot be left to our own devices. This lie is what they use to justify their existence and position to us. This is why they spend so much time filling our heads with nonsense; at school, through the media, from the church and government etc., to keep us feeling dependant on them. We believe that people are capable of living together in peace, running their own lives and making their own decisions and enjoying it! We could go further and say as we pointed out in earlier chapters that we have so much to gain from coming together in such a way that we would inevitably do so out of self-interest. We have often tried throughout history. The reason we do not live in a better world now is not because we are 'bad', but because we are prevented from doing so. We will look a bit more at whether we are going to be 'good enough' to have a new better world.

● Changes

By the time we are on the verge of this new world we will have had to do a number of things, besides bury the ruling class and their lackeys! The things that our class will have done will have brought them to this point and will have changed them in the process *(refer to the previous chapter)*. Before and during the revolution there will have been intense activity in our class. This will be both organisational and political. New ways of running society and viewing the world will have emerged. We see several things as vital for us to have achieved for the new world to succeed.

● Education

Learning about uprisings and revolutions of the past so that mistakes are not repeated. Finding out how the State and capitalism operated and looking at how different forms of organising can ensure revolutionary gains are not lost.

● Understanding

Finding out about not only different societies but also examining different attitudes and cultures and how irrational divisions are implanted in our minds to divide us such as racism and sexism.

● Self-Management

To enjoy the control over our own lives and the shared collective power to alter our futures and make the physical world a better place to live. This will mean breaking with our conditioned reliance on officials and bosses and 'experts' making decisions for us. This maybe hard at first, but history shows we quickly develop a passion for it!

● Solidarity

Instead of being forced to work in competition against each other, locally and internationally, for the benefit of the bosses. Our actions in the community and at work will not be viewed through the blinkered eyes of capitalism in terms of how much money or muscle we have, but in terms of our input into society for the benefit of all including ourselves. Instead selfishness, competition and bigotry will be replaced by awareness, understanding and an attitude best described by the saying "All for one, and one for all".

So what happens when some individuals or groups put in nothing and take out as much as they can in terms of acquiring goods and gaining power, or engage in anti-social behaviour? They will have broken the bond of solidarity that ties them to the rest of us and will have taken the first steps to re-building the old world. We are all aware of the dangers of this happening. As we have already indicated the strengths of the political ideas and organisational structures will have been built up before and during a revolution and will be the foundation of the success of the new world. But solidarity will need to be argued for before, during and after the revolution.

● The Defence of the Revolution

The leftovers of the old world will not be ignored. Those following cruel and bigoted religions, fascists or Leninist-type ideologies will not be ignored. They can run but they won't be able to hide from us! Too many uprisings have been crushed or subverted by such ideas. We've no intention of letting this happen again. The best defence against such a threat is to place power and knowledge in the hands of so many that these new bosses are starved of the ignorant followers they need to take them to power. In a very real sense we see ourselves as finishing the job our class started in Russia during the February

uprising of 1917, that was interrupted by the Bolshevik party, with the loss of many fine people.

There will of course be workers militia's in existence to defend the revolution if there is a continuing civil war. If parts of the planet are still occupied by the capitalists we can expect them to attack us with the aid of any remaining nation-states. The need for a world wide revolution cannot, we believe, be overstated. Revolution in one country or region will not be enough, except as a temporary situation. To survive we will have to wipe capitalism and the State off the face of the Earth or it will destroy us. The courage of those who have gone before us, and of those who are currently fighting at 'home' and 'abroad' are an inspiration to us all. We intend to use all our wit, humour and strength in this fight.

●SUMMING UP

We believe the benefits, either real or potential, that the new world presents to our class are so great that movement towards it, with help from organisations such as ours, will sooner or later become unstoppable.

Despite this and the revolutionary vision that is alive and kicking in so many peoples hearts we often hear that the revolution will be spoilt by 'others'. This idea that there are loads of people who wouldn't accept a good thing when they saw it, we don't agree with. As we have shown we expect people to change as the false society of capitalism and the State is dismantled and destroyed. We have given some pointers to the basic changes that we can expect to see and how, if you care to look, you can see the outlines of the new world in the struggles of the past and the present. In this chapter we've not tried to answer a series of detailed questions. We don't have a set of smart answers as to how exactly the new world will operate nor do we want to. Unlike the ruling class, and those who aspire to be on the Left, we do not underestimate the imagination, ingenuity, common sense, humour and courage of our class.

To sum up the basics of the new world again: we will abolish artificial divisions, class and money. We will encourage knowledge, understanding, self-management and solidarity. By doing so our class will provide the means of making a world human community.

● CONCLUSION

Greedy rich money men, politicians, paid thugs, lies, bigotry, economic slavery and mental and physical violence is what the old world is all about. The new world will see the divisions of the old world fully destroyed during and after a revolution. There will be no division between work and leisure. Our daily lives will become filled with interest, pleasure and challenges, in stark contrast to the lives that many of us lead today. We see no transitionary worker's State this time around as the Left does, we have learnt the lessons of history. Freedom, solidarity, equality, justice and security will not be empty slogans but the day-to-day reality. We will realise a society based around,

"From each according to their abilities, to each according to their needs".

THIS WORLD IS OURS FOR THE TAKING. THE NEW WORLD IS OURS FOR THE MAKING.

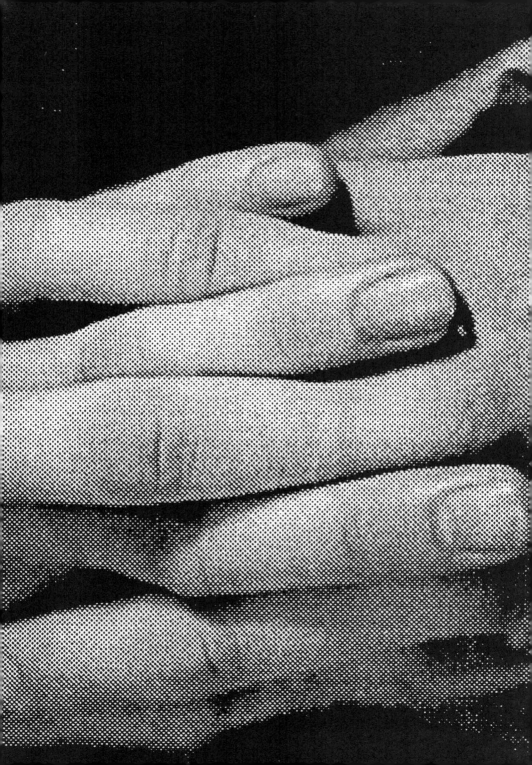

*"Remember your hardships and keep up your struggle,
The wheel will turn for you,
By the strength of your hands and hardness of your fists."*
Mary MacPherson, Isle of Skye, Scotland in the
19th century - translated from the Gaelic in the play
"The Cheviot the Stag and the Black Oil" by John
McGrath.

Section Headings
- Introduction.
- What a Revolutionary Organisation is Like.
- What is not a Revolutionary Organisation.
- Summing Up.

● INTRODUCTION

There will be more than one organisation. This is taken for
granted. In fact it is in our tactical interests to encourage similar groups
as ours to start and grow. This should become clear from what follows
below. In revolutionary periods in history all sorts of movements and
organisations are thrown up. Some will be good, others will be bad. All
sorts of shifting social alliances will be made as the course of the
revolution progresses. We must be prepared to hard sell our ideas in
this period (and before!) and not just trust to spontaneity to pull us
through as some of the anarchists seem to think. This section is
informed by "The Organisational Platform of the Libertarian
Communists", written by a group of exiled Russian anarchists drawing
on their experiences in the Russian revolution of 1917.

● Organisation or Movement?

As will become clear below we see organisations like the Class War
Federation as playing a part, with others, in the creation and defence

of a revolutionary movement within the working class. This movement will be a strong and diverse collection of the revolutionary sections of our class under nobody's control but their own. Yet this movement will also have to be politically coherent. It must have a certain minimum of shared ideas. The Class War Federation and similar organisations exist to bring about this situation. This is the meaning and spirit of this chapter and the rest of this book.

● Why do we need Organisations?

The short answer is that if people are to achieve any objective involving a number of others then some kind of organisation is necessary whether that objective is growing corn, building a house or destroying the State and capitalism. For any of these things to be done the people involved must know what they want to achieve and how they are going to do it, wishing it is so will not do anything. What follows examines the types of organisations that can be of use to the working class - and those that can't.

● WHAT A REVOLUTIONARY ORGANISATION IS LIKE

● Aims of the Organisation

To work as a group of people who come together to further the interests of the working class. Specifically, they aim by their propaganda work and other activities in the class to help their class reach a position where they are in a condition to start on the road to revolution. The priority is to aid the class to 'manage itself' in its revolutionary activities. The organisation is not trying to be a new set of bosses as the Leninist parties do. We are aware that where as for us the autonomy and self-management of the working class is an end in itself, for much of the Left this is only a means to an end i.e. taking power by taking over the State. A revolutionary organisation believes in our class's ability to lead itself and works towards this end. In doing this the organisation is not afraid of pointing out to the class what it believes is right at any moment. The aim is to talk as equals with respect to the rest of our class.

Obviously influential figures and organisations are thrown up by the working class in struggle, and they do push for certain objectives. This is to be expected and their relationship to the class is central to assessing their value. In short they have to encourage their class to 'do-it-themselves'. A good example from history would be the Ukrainian anarchist and insurgent movement 1917-22. The military wing defeated both the Red Army, and the counter revolutionary White Army. They did not, as a result, expect to rule socially and made this clear. Instead they worked closely with the local Soviets on social matters, and regarded themselves as the armed wing of the working class and had enough sense to realise that the social and economic part of the revolution was as important as its military defence. For more information see "History of the Machnovist Movement" by Peter Arshinov.

● Strategy of the Organisation

The aim of any strategy is to play a part in the process of creating a large section of the working class that is political and in control of it's own activities. This strategy is guided by examining where the working class are in reality, not where we would like them to be, a failure of the Left in Britain to date. By looking at the condition of our class we come to conclusions about what we should do. In Britain basic propaganda work needs to be done now. The following list identifies some of the things our class requires to be able to take the road to revolution, already mentioned in Chapter Five. This list therefore becomes part of the strategic objectives that we aim to achieve by our work as individuals and as an organisation.

● Needs of the Working Class

Identity. The working class need to assert their own identity in opposition to that which they are 'given' today. It will need to be up to date and free of sentimental and patronising images.

Pride. Instead of being persuaded to feel inferior and only experiencing pride on the terms of the ruling class, such as love of Royalty and British nationalism, our class need to be proud of themselves and their achievements.

Solidarity. In place of snobbery and competition, the older and deeper values of unity and common interest need to be retrieved and stressed at very opportunity.

Culture. The emergence of a genuine working class culture where the above ideas and values are combined with a sense of history, self confidence and a vision of the future. This would replace a lot of what at present is passed off as 'working class culture'. Out would go racism, sexism, macho-shite, bigoted ideas about gays and lesbians, the urge to dominate and bully, the need to be ordered around, ignorance and selfish ambitions.

Self Management. The idea of managing ourselves would have to be taken up in our communities and workplaces.

Internationalism. It is crucial for the British working class to get over its legacy of Imperialism.

Support. Wide spread support for the above ideas and values through the working class - not necessarily a majority, but enough to make change and revolution possible. The identifying of those sections of our class where this support can be built becomes part of the organisation's strategy.

● Practice of the Organisation

This is determined by the aims and strategy. It has been said that what a revolutionary group has got to offer the rest of the working class can be found by looking at its internal workings. The organisation must

have;

● Internal democracy with all posts being re-callable. This means that people who are elected to do certain jobs such as being secretaries, membership organisers, editors etc. can and will be replaced at any time. The aim is that power over the organisation stays at the local levels, not in some elite central group.

● Clear political ideas and aims.

● Clear membership - we have to know who is in and who is not and importantly what the basis of that membership is; i.e. a certain basic grasp of our ideas and a level of commitment in effort and money.

● Comradeship and the ability to care.

● An effective system for members to educate themselves and pass on basic skills like writing articles, public speaking, propaganda, fighting and publicity skills etc. Without this the organisation will wither and die physically and politically.

The "Platform Of The Libertarian Communists" referred to earlier makes some exact suggestions for organisation and methods. Here they are in boiled down form. We see no need to disagree;

● Theoretical unity.
● Tactical unity or the collective method of action.
● Collective responsibility.
● Federalism.

THEORETICAL UNITY. Theory (ideas) represents the force which directs the activity of persons and organisations along a defined path towards a determined goal. It also binds the individuals and groups together into a more effective force. A certain minimum agreement on ideas is obviously essential.

TACTICAL UNITY OR THE COLLECTIVE METHOD OF ACTION. A common tactical line in the movement is of decisive importance for the existence of the "organisation". It removes the disastrous effect of several tactics in opposition to one another. It concentrates all the forces of the organisation on its objectives.

Put bluntly this means the organisation must know what it is trying to achieve and how. Incredibly, many groupings in the Left and anarchist movement do not know this beyond a vague desire to do something 'good'. It is essential that the organisation has a strategy for achieving its objectives based on realistic objectives for short and medium term goals. Self management starts at home!

COLLECTIVE RESPONSIBILITY. The entire organisation will be responsible for the political and revolutionary activity of each member; therefore each member will be accountable for their actions to the rest of the organisation. The aim of the organisation is to do its work as effectively as possible. This means out in the open public activity. This sort of work carries risks of its own with it and people should consider how it affects other parts of their lives before getting involved.

FEDERALISM. Anarchism, against centralism, has always professed and defended the principle of federalism, which reconciles the independence and initiative of individuals and the organisation with service to the common cause. Federalism is a way of social organising that brings together independent groups for commonly agreed purposes and agree to co-operate with majority decisions. In this set up, each person and group at all levels has the freedom to argue their position and, if they choose, to leave the Federation altogether.

The groundwork for this new way of organising will be laid before and during the revolution, as is indicated in the chapters on Class Struggle and Revolution. The emphasis is going to be on practical self management; the need to respect though not necessarily blindly follow the wishes of the majority, the use of delegates who are recallable instantly to represent our views to other groups and free access to information. But quite often, the federalist principle has been deformed: it has often been understood as the right, above all, to manifest one's ego, without obligation to account for duties as regards the organisation.

This false interpretation disorganised our movement in the past. It is time to put an end to it in a firm and irreversible manner. Federalism will only become reality, rather than fiction or illusion, on the condition that all participants fulfil most completely the duties undertaken, and conform to communal decisions.

●WHAT IS NOT A REVOLUTIONARY ORGANISATION

It is not composed of people who follow the teachings of Lenin, Trotsky, or Mao who all believed in taking control of the State with a vanguard party on behalf of the working class. It does not believe it is possible to use the State to destroy capitalism or even to work towards that end, unlike the British Left parties such as Militant, the Socialist

Workers Party (SWP) or the Revolutionary Communist Party (RCP).

It is not composed of middle class people who act out their traditional roles of domination and management of working class people who are members, as in the SWP, or controlled by an upper class group with a working class membership such as Militant.

What makes the Left parties like those mentioned above so unworthy of support is, apart from with their obsession with their own unique fitness to lead, the fact that they all claim to have the one and only, definitive and correct understanding of the works of Marx, Engels, Lenin, and often Trotsky. They all believe that they and only they have the correct understanding of so-called "scientific socialism". There must be upwards of a dozen organisations making this claim, yet the only thing they have in common is that they all detest each other, and that each believes only they have the right interpretation and everyone else is wrong. If any theory is capable of so many wide spread and contradictory interpretations, then we should look on its claim to scientific exactitude with the greatest scepticism.

Neither is a revolutionary organisation composed of working class people who are full of sentimental and moralistic nonsense about the class struggle and themselves. Such a group inevitably ends getting led around by a charismatic figure and achieves nothing. Nor is the organisation an alliance of single issue groups and individuals with little grasp of class politics, something which has bedevilled anarchism in the UK from the start.

● Anarchism

In its true form it is the same as communism, coming from the same tradition; that of working class resistance to oppression. However, anarchism in the UK and elsewhere has tended, over time, to be hijacked by the middle class (because of its stress on the individual) and used to justify doing nothing. The Russian anarchist movement was criticised for doing the same thing during the Russian revolution by anarchists in the Ukraine. These criticisms apply as much today as they did then, we think it well worth repeating them.

"We are obliged to state that the Russian anarchists remained in their circles and slept through a mass movement of paramount importance. But at the same time, we discover that this deplorable situation is not accidental, but that it has very specific causes, which we will now consider.

The majority of our anarchist theorists have their origins in the intelligentsia. This circumstance is very significant. While standing under the banner of anarchism, many of them are not able to break altogether with the psychological context from which they emerged.

Very few amongst the isolated anarchists found in themselves the necessary sensitivity and courage to recognise that this movement was the one anarchism had been anticipating for many years - those who did rushed to join it.

An even more important aspect of this helplessness and inactivity of the anarchists is the confusion in anarchist theory and the organisational chaos in anarchist ranks.

Thus many anarchists devoted their energies to the question of whether the task of anarchism is the liberation of classes, humanity, or of the personality. The question is empty, but is based on some unclear anarchist positions and provides a broad field for abuse of anarchist thought and practice.

An even greater field for abuse is created by the unclear anarchist theory of individual freedom. Those who do not know the passion of the revolution, who are most concerned with their "I", understand this idea in their own fashion. Whenever the question of practical anarchist *organisation or the question of organisation with a serious intent is posed, they hang on to the theory of individual liberty and using this as a basis oppose all organisation and escape from all responsibility. The ideas and actions of anarchists are thus pulverised to the point of derangement.*

For dozens of years the Russian anarchists have suffered from the disease of disorganisation. Thus when the mass movement rose from the depths of the people, the anarchists showed themselves completely unprepared, spineless and weak.

In our opinion this is temporary. Anarchism is not mysticism: it is not a discourse on beauty; it is not a cry of despair. Its greatness is due, above all, to its devotion to the cause of oppressed humanity. It carries within itself the truth, and the aspirations of the masses, and is today the only social doctrine the masses can count on in their struggle. But this is not enough. Anarchism needs to go to the masses and merge with them."

"History of the Makhnovist Movement" - Peter Arshinov.

● Tourists

In the British Left and anarchist movements exists a wandering tribe of individuals who drift from group to group. Some are full of intellectual rigour and passion who will argue day and night for a precise point but do nothing. One example is that some will argue that it is wrong to be involved in anti-fascist work because it implies support for capitalism of which fascism is just another organisational form. Others are people often displaced socially by previous unfortunate experiences. We do not intend to become an 'orphanage' for such people.

● The Bank

A revolutionary organisation is like a bank. To survive, most of its members must be in credit in terms of money and activity. Obviously there are always some of us who at times may get 'overdrawn'. But when too many are overdrawn the bank closes. What do we mean by overdrawn? If an organisation is attracting people who take more out than they put in, then it is finished. This a particular failing of the traditional anarchist and Left revolutionary scene in Britain with its emphasis on lifestyle.

We all get down in the dumps at times, stress is very common in our society and this is where comradeship and caring are important. But if an organisation is attracting people who demand or require a lot of support then it is doomed. We are not a therapy group. Sometimes you have to be cruel to be kind!

● Missionaries

This refers to some common tendencies in the British Left which we mean to avoid. On the one hand are the cynical Left like the Revolutionary Communist Party, Socialist Workers Party etc. who will pick up an issue and run with it until they can gain no more from it in terms of membership, money, influence and publicity. They will descend on a struggle or issue and milk it dry for their own interests and then piss off!

Sometimes the change of party line that comes down from central headquarters is so rapid that the activists on the ground are left mouthing the wrong slogans; this is particularly true of the Socialist Workers Party.

Then there is an attitude common in the anarchist scene which is well intentioned but ineffective and can be called "the must do something syndrome". An understandable reaction to an unjust world. This often comes unstuck through a lack of understanding of the beast it is up against, capitalism and the class system. Worthy and imaginative initiatives such as the community cafes of the 1980's tend to fall apart because they are an alliance of single issues politics without a common thread. Much of the activity is geared to making those involved feel better.

Even in many class struggle anarchist groups this tendency is still strong, with effort devoted solely to various campaigns. The reasons for expending large amounts of effort in this way again boils down to making those concerned feel better. As the saying goes, they cannot see the wood for the trees.

Neither of these kinds of missionary tend to stay around long. On the other hand we in the Class War Federation and similar organisations have a clear and straightforward aim as we have outlined above. We are going to build organisations which will have in-depth support and popularity in this country and around the world, and whose groups and activities will be dispersed throughout our class where it counts. We will make sure we have the clarity of thought and determination of action to succeed in our objectives, which are to play our part in creating a revolutionary movement in society. We intend to be around for as long as it takes.

● Workers and Intellectuals in the Organisation

This is an old chestnut and often the cause of friction. The Italian anarchist Maltesta deals with it well;

'We have no 'working class' prejudices, no preferences for the manual worker because he is a manual worker, and above all no admiration for the uneducated and the illiterates, who, nevertheless, have the valid excuse, that their condition is not their fault".

Errico Malatesta.

Contrast this to the anti-intellectualism of many contemporary anarchists and socialists, many of whom are from upper class backgrounds and have had the best education available. But Malatesta continues;

"On the other hand we know that most of the so-called intellectuals are, by reason of their education, their family background, their class prejudices, tied to the Establishment, and tend to want the subjection of the masses to their will.

We accept the intellectuals with pleasure and without suspicion when they fuse with the working class, when they join the people without the pretensions to command; without a patronising air of condescension, but with the open mind of someone coming amidst brothers and sisters to repay them a debt they have contracted in educating themselves, which in most cases is at the expense of the children of those whose work has produced their means of education".

Errico Maltesta - Italian Anarchist; Umanita Nova 1921.

The 'dictatorship of the intellectual' is not something we intend to copy from the left-wing parties. Our aim is to make everyone an intellectual.

● Horses for Courses

There will be many different groups and individuals in the same organisation and the wider mass movement. They will have different experiences and approaches and each will be good at different things.

But how will they work together and treat each other? The following quote from "The Eclipse and Re-emergence of the Communist Movement" gives us an idea.

"Some groups are a more 'direct' expression of the proletariat. Others maybe more 'dogmatic' as they try to grasp the whole historical movement. Origins and experiences are very different. Revolutionaries are able to understand and criticize each other. Communication is vital. Those who are only interested in theory, as well as those who are only interested in organising others' activity, stand outside the communist movement."

- Barrot and Martin.

In other words one of the essential characteristics of a revolutionary is the desire and ability to understand others in different situations and from different backgrounds.

● SUMMING UP

So a revolutionary organisation is not a cosy social club for refugees from the real world, like so much of the left-wing and anarchist scene in this country.

The organisation and the people in it must have; the clarity of ideas to cut through the ruling class's attacks, toughness and strange as it may seem, the ability to care. One of the 'perks' of the job is the increased self-respect that comes from fighting back, comrades you can depend on, and ideas that help you see through the bad times, and last but not least being in an organisation with a sense of humour!

Appendix

A brief history of capitalism

In the 1700's and the century before, the ideas of the 'economy of scale', it being cheaper to make a lot of one thing in one place, together with a desire to control a semi-rural work force, were the driving forces behind the first factories. At the same time dramatic changes in agriculture, such as crop rotation and landlords enclosing fields that were previously communal with walls or hedges, created vast profits for the landowners (mostly the aristocracy), who eventually invested it in new industries.

This first great accumulation of capital, at our expense, was one of the events that marked the start of capitalism proper and set the tone for its later development. These changes also displaced many people from the land and created great poverty. As was pointed out in Chapter One these developments were paralleled by an expansion abroad by the European capitalists in their search for gold and silver to fuel the increasing demand for these metals as a means of storing their growing capital. It is from around this time that capitalist imperialism properly gets off the grounds.

The working class resisted but eventually the economic power of the masters and a State penal code that was one of the cruelest and brutal in the world won the day. For example, you could be hung for stealing a handkerchief, if it was owned by a 'gentleman'. This period was crucial to hammering out the present characteristics of the English working class. The way the law was used was very important in this process. It was a mixture of terror and benevolence and explains much of the present attitudes in our class. Here is a good summary of some of the methods employed;

"The law was used not only to privatise as property what had been commonly enjoyed, but also, and inseperably, to render as crimes what had been customary rights, and to execute, transport or condemn to the hulks those subsequently criminalised. Between 1688 and 1820 the number of capital offences grew from around 50 to over 200; the bulk of the additions concerned offences against property. By 1740 it was a capital offence to steal property worth one shilling. Food rioters and machine breakers faced the death sentence and enclosure rioters transportation. The Black Act of 1723 created fifty new offences at a stroke.

As to enactment, much remained in the hands of JPs - nakedly representing gentry interests. Assizes - the only point of contact for most people with the central State - were occasions of great pomp and ceremonial. The awesome centrepiece of the assizes was the ritual surrounding the pronouncement of the death sentence. Executions were public spectacles, and the ritual of public execution was a necessary part of a system of social discipline where a great deal depended on theatre. The strict application of the 'law' and importantly the dispensation of 'mercy' helped over time to persuade people that the law was above everybody and fair. Which of course it is not.

Estimates are that maybe 20% of those convicted of capital offences were sentenced to death and of those just half were actually executed. The word of a 'gentleman' could influence a jury not to convict or a judge to recommend pardons or leniency. This helped to create the mental structure of paternalism, cementing dependence with gratitude and qualifying the impersonal rigour of the law. We have something far stronger here than coercion alone."

    - from "The Great Arch" by Corrigan and Sayer.

It is worth noting that the introduction of capitalism was fiercely resisted by the peasants and early factory workers. This resistance

was overcome by extreme brutality - famine, massacres, murder, torture and transportation. This is the real history of capitalism. The people chucked off the land and out of the small cottage workshops and terrorised by this legal system were to become the industrial working class of the 19th century. They formed the vast pool of people who had nothing except the ability to work, called the 'proletariat', an awkward sounding word derived from Latin meaning someone without property but one notch above being a slave! From this great mass of dispossessed people were recruited the workers the capitalists required.

The introduction of machines such as Arkwright's spinning jenny, Watt's steam engine and Akroyd's powerlooms and the dividing of labour into narrow repetitive actions following the teachings of the economic philosophers such as Adam Smith, reduced the role of the workers to machine feeders and minders or just 'factory hands'. This was again stiffly resisted with machine breaking, armed rebellion and executions of mill-owners. Again the resistance was defeated by a mixture of military means and divide and rule propaganda such as loyalism and sexism. The economic power of the masters and merchants that was protected by the State was used to hold whole communities to ransom until they adopted new methods of work, often at the point of starvation. The city and factory age of capitalism had arrived.

The late 18th and early 19th century was a period of great brutality and squalor for the victims of capitalism. It would be fair to say that our people resisted tooth and nail against being turned into "the working class". Under the new regime, their standard of living dropped with drastically lower wages than before. This in turn produced another great accumulation of capital that went to fuel the economic engine of capitalism in its growth. Here is an examples of what was involved; Cobbett, a social commentator talking of the weavers in Halifax in 1832 observed;

"It is truly lamentable to behold so many thousands of men who formerly earned 20 to 30 shillings a week, now compelled to live on 5 or 4 shillings and even less a week".

from "The Making of the English Working Class" - E.P. Thompson.

This well and truly marked the end of the traditions of feudalism in the economic life of society, although it lingered on in the legal system with its emphasis on benevolence. It was replaced with the ideas of classical liberalism. The old paternalistic views were now those of a small minority. This new set of ideas, or ideology, was given its clearest expression in 1776 in Adam Smith's "Wealth of Nations" which reflected the needs of the new capitalist order and totally broke the hold of the older views. The new capitalists needed to break the restraints on their production and trade that feudalism had maintained and Adam Smith's work gave them their theoretical justification. At the heart of this were four main assumptions about people. They were considered to be lazy, selfish, cunning and generally independent of society. This is really a description of the capitalist's own attitudes and values. In other words they assumed the world to be a mirror of themselves. This is typical of the arrogance of the ruling class, and one of their weaknesses.

Smith's work also assumed that an economy was made up of many small enterprises, so no individual company could exercise any significant influence on the market, hence his idea of a free market. With the growing concentration of capitalism into bigger companies you would think his work would be redundant but not so. Much of the history of economics since has been the patching up of Smith's ideas. From this period in working class history we can see the origins of the present Labour Party and trade union tradition, the Tolpuddle martyrs. The name says it all, "Martyrs", a forelock tugging bunch of religious berks who got transported for trying to form a union. They were so wet the ruling class let them come back. We draw our inspiration from the Luddites, the "Captain Swing" rural fighters and the Naval and Army mutineers of the period as well as the London Mob. And of course the Paris Commune, who gave Karl Marx the biggest shock of his life. In 1871 the Paris workers and some of the middle class rose in revolt - they were brutally suppressed with over 20,000 killed.

But by the mid 19th century the British ruling class had succeeded in constructing the present structure of society as we know it. The efforts of social engineering by the Tories under Thatcher were a pale shadow of the events of the 18th and 19th century. We still live in the shadow of this 'Great Arch' of oppression that they finished building in the 19th century.

"In these years (the 19th century) the Great Arch of the modern ruling class was finally finished, many of the bricks marked with the graffiti of the vanquished, and much blood, most of it foreign, mixed with the cement."

- from "The Great Arch" by Corrigan and Sayer.

Ireland

This is a practical example of colonialism and a divided working class right on our door step.

At the moment in what is only technically a part of the UK, a section of the working class is resisting the rule of the British ruling class. An area about the size of Yorkshire with a population less than that of Birmingham has fought the British State to a standstill. There are approximately 10,000 regular frontline troops from mainland Britain garrisoned here. They support a local police force numbering about 10,000 that is heavily armed (pistols, rifles, machine guns, plastic bullets, gas, armoured cars etc.).

In addition there is a locally raised regiment of part time soldiers that only serves in Northern Ireland; the Ulster Defence Regiment, a kind of local official vigilante force. They also number around 10,000 with standard army equipment. Support is given by the Royal Navy and RAF. Elite units such as the SAS, SBS, Marines and the Paras' are also employed at different times.

What we have here is a war against the British State and a civil war in our class right under our noses. If we are serious about what we believe, we must look at Northern Ireland and draw some conclusions. After all we can hardly ignore a war on our doorstep. Bearing in mind that this situation is definitely a colonial one we recommend that you refer to Chapter One to get a background to what colonialism is and its effects on our class in general and the problems that nationalist struggles raise for us.

● UNDERSTANDING NORTHERN IRELAND

We have tried to keep this as brief and clear as possible. There are some excellent books on Ireland and we strongly recommend you read them *(please refer to the booklist)*. This only skims over recent Irish history.

Once, all of Ireland was owned by the British. They took and maintained control with all the usual cruelty of imperialism. The Irish experience is similar to that of the Africans, even down to famine and slavery - a sixth of the population were sold as slaves to the Americas in Cromwell's time. Eventually a popular rising resulted in the British being forced out of the Southern part of Ireland in 1922 after years of bitter war. This was followed by a civil war in Ireland between those who wanted to continue the fight against Britain to retake Northern Ireland, who came to be known as Republicans and those who wanted to settle for what they had won, who came to be known as 'Free Staters'. The Free Staters won and Ireland was partitioned into two sections, North and South.

We should look more closely at this northern section of Ireland and why it came into existence.

In the 19th century the northern part of Ireland along with Scotland and South Wales came to be the most heavily industrialised parts of the British Empire and the source of fabulous wealth for the ruling class. The history of Irish resistance to British rule had been a long one and the ruling class had for sometime been trying to divide the workforce in order to subdue them.

After the abortive attempt at revolution by the United Irishmen in 1798, in which the Protestants were prominent, the British resolved to foster divisions between the Catholics and the Protestants. The basis of this division was to be the one thing that each had that was different, their religion.

This gathered speed in the North where the ruling class were becoming increasingly vulnerable to the effects of a united working class in the mass employment of the area's industries. Fiery Protestant preachers were shipped in from Scotland, and Protestants began to be given more preference for jobs and land. The Orange Order became a tool to bring the Protestants in the North closer to their masters. Ironically the Order was founded by Anglican Protestants, those from the English elite looking to England, and at first excluded the Northern Irish Presbyterian Protestants, those from the Scottish Tradition, because they were too democratic and too 'Irish'!

This religious or sectarian division was whipped up more strongly towards the end of the 19th century as the Irish agitated for 'Home Rule'. In the first few years of the 20th century the Irish working classes were involved in massive strikes both in the North and the South. The ruling class in the North could see which way the wind was blowing and determined that they were going to hang on to their wealthy corner of Ireland because they owed their wealth to being a part of the British Empire and did not want to become part of a much poorer Independent State.

Their propaganda machine went into top gear to whip up division and hatred between the Catholics and Protestants. At this time Ireland was experiencing some of the biggest strikes Europe has ever seen. Loyalism and Unionism were the names given to the movements they created to protect their power; Loyalism, as in loyal to the monarch, the head of the British State, and Unionism as in the 'Union' of Northern Ireland with the rest of the 'United Kingdom' the UK.

In July 1912 the Ulster Unionists and Orange Order were to declare "holy war" against the Catholics. (This has a strange ring to it these days when we are told that sort of thing only happens in the Middle East). Nearly a quarter of a million Ulster Unionists pledged to fight Home Rule by means of arms. Incredibly they also stated that if Home Rule was imposed on them they would not stay in an independent Ireland but would ask the German Kaiser to rule them as their Monarch. The Ulster ruling class was quite prepared to join the German State to protect their interests, which illustrates nicely the hypocrisy of their patriotism.

Most of the support for Home Rule, not surprisingly, was in the South of Ireland. But this political difference was also based on economic differences. The South contained petty capitalists and an ambitious and political middle class. This group could not develop their businesses because the might of the British economy was too competitive and too close. What this group needed was protection from the British economy.

The Northern industrialists on the other hand owed their position to having access to Britains imperial markets and power. Ireland had two sets of capitalists at different stages of development. This fact was to dominate the life of Ireland until the 1960's.

● The South of Ireland Since 1922

The Southern 'Free State' of Ireland had been achieved at the cost of terrible suffering yet the influence of English capital was as strong as ever. It was just the local management that had changed. This process was to be repeated throughout the British Empire. James Connoly, the Irish socialist, foresaw this. Writing in the Irish paper "Shan Van Vocht", he made what was to become a profound prophecy for the modern Irish State.

"If you remove the English army tomorrow and hoist the green flag

over Dublin Castle, unless you set about the organisation of the Socialist Republic, your efforts would be in vain. England would still rule you. She would rule you through her capitalists, through her landlords, through her financiers, through her array of commercial and individual institutions she has planted in this country."

From "Shan Van Vocht".

In this way Britain has remained one of the leading imperialist powers in the world, while many of her citizens think that the 'Empire' is a thing of the past.

● THE NORTHERN IRISH STATE SINCE 1922

After the partition of Ireland the Northern Industrialists were given their own little 'parliament'; Stormont. This wealthy little corner of Britain was theirs to run as they liked with little or no interference from London and the Orange Order was central to keeping control in this

small 'Statelet'. What this meant was the systematic terrorising of the Catholic community by a heavily armed police and paramilitary force (the notorious A, B and C Specials), that was entirely Protestant. The economic attractions of this colonial set-up were still strong. With a divided working class they could make more money by paying lower wages and providing less services from local government.

Northern Ireland had and still has some of the worst housing in Europe. The prejudice and bigotry that was whipped up to protect the Northern ruling class had to be continued for economic and political reasons. The divisions it created helped keep industry in the North profitable longer by keeping wages low, keeping the Catholics down kept the Protestants happy with their lot, which was hardly any better. The situation has close parallels with the racism against blacks in the UK, which also is intended to keep the white working class happy with their lot. As Karl Marx might point out, the rise of Unionism and Loyalism is a clear example of political and social events being determined by economic forces. Later though the reverse was to happen. As they say "the tail wagged the dog".

By the 1960's, with the wave of optimism that swept the industrial world and inspired by the black civil rights movements of the USA, people began to protest in Northern Ireland. Their demands were for things like housing, education, jobs and the vote (at this time there was a property qualification to receive the vote, this effectively denied the vote to many Catholics). The Irish working classes, Catholic and Protestant, took to the streets to voice their desires for change and a better way of life. The response was brutal. The demonstrators were beaten off the streets by the police and Protestant gangs. Worse was to come. The police in Ulster had pistols, rifles and sub-machine guns as standard issue. They together with Protestant gangs went into Catholic areas and shot people at random and burned down whole streets at a time.

Random killing and torture of Catholics became the pattern, (the largest mass murders in Britain were carried out by the 'Shankhill Butchers' a Loyalist gang). In response whole Catholic areas became no-go zones for the police such as 'Free Derry'. These survived until the London government took power from the local government and imposed direct rule from Westminster and sent in troops and tanks to smash them. Forced to defend themselves the Catholics drew on the old Republican traditions to build community organisations that could withstand these attacks.

Since then the Catholics in the North of Ireland have continued to resist and as was pointed out earlier have held the British State to a stalemate.

● The Present

The cost to the Catholic community has been enormous yet they have refused, to date, to swallow any of the deals that the British have offered them. From their point of view there can be no going back to things as they were and that means breaking the power of the 'Orange State' of Ulster and its military machine. Underneath all the political manoeuvres, the British to date have been unable to make the Loyalist ruling class give ground.

This is because the Loyalist/Unionist/Orange machine of bigotry and privilege has taken on a life of its own independent of the economic interests that created it in the first place. The economy of Northern Ireland was in steep decline in the 1960's. Now it is in a shambles propped up by money from London. Yet Loyalism continues like a zombie unaware that it is dead. The tail is well and truly wagging the dog.

To the British ruling class Ulster is a running sore. It has to support the local Loyalist elite who are in reality no longer of any use to them. Yet they cannot ditch them. Why, you might well ask. Why not pull out? There are a number of reasons.

No State will voluntarily give up a piece of its territory. It is bad for its image elsewhere. All States are artificial. Giving up Northern Ireland would raise tensions elsewhere in the 'United' Kingdom that are at present under control, e.g. Scotland, Wales, the North etc. It would be also seen as a sign of weakness and decline of the whole British ruling class by other ruling classes in the world. As one Tory MP once expressed it:

"If we lose in Belfast, we may have to fight in Brixton and Birmingham".

- John Biggs-Davidson.

The normal pattern in colonial conflicts like this is to pull out and pass on power to a local power group with whom the old colonial power feels it can do business, as with the 'Free Staters' in the South of Ireland in 1922. There is no group in Northern Ireland that the British can pass power on to, at the moment. This is their objective though, even if it means creating a new power group in Northern Ireland. This is what the British ruling class have been doing for generations elsewhere.

To pull out of Northern Ireland without some sort of local settlement would de-stabilise the south of Ireland. Without British support the Orange elite would be defeated militarily without doubt. The aim of the Sinn Fein and IRA etc. is to unify Ireland. The Southern ruling class would be very unhappy about this as they hate the Republicans as much as the Loyalists do! The likely outcome would be some sort of conflict if not civil war.

The prospect of that happening off the coast of Britain is very disturbing to the British and international ruling classes.

● THE PROTESTANTS

As was pointed out earlier the present strength of Loyalism and Unionism in the Protestant community owes its origins to the desire of the Northern Ireland ruling class to protect their very profitable part of Ireland. They weakened working class unity by whipping up sectarian hatred between Catholic and Protestant. This meant portraying the Catholics as the enemy, i.e. as savages and godless. The threat used against the Protestants was that the Catholics would rise up and sweep them out of Ulster if they were given a chance.

This was backed up with a warped and distorted history to encourage a siege mentality in the Protestant community. So the Catholics became the scapegoat for all the problems of the Protestants like unemployment, low wages and the housing shortage. In this way the Protestants were persuaded that their best interest was to side with the Orange boss class. The Catholics are used and attacked in Northern Ireland by the ruling class in the same way as are the blacks in Britain.

If sectarian hatred was the method the ruling elite in Northern Ireland used to divide the working class, then the Orange Order was the means that was used to bind the Protestant working class to their masters. Membership in the 1960s numbered about 200,000. To get a job on the local council, in the civil service and many industries membership of the Order was useful, and often necessary. The more important and sensitive the job, the more important it became to be a member of the Order. For higher placed jobs individuals had to belong to more extreme branches of the order like the 'Apprentice Boys' or the

'Black Preceptory'.

Even though many Protestants feel that the Order is outdated and backwards the benefits of membership were, and are, real enough to make it worth while joining. Giving preference to Protestants for jobs, housing and land is the economic cement that holds the walls of the Orange State of Northern Ireland together. Ironically, it is because the working class in Northern Ireland are so divided that the whole of that class are so badly off when compared to those in Britain in terms of wages, housing and unemployment.

Despite all this the Protestants have at times come together with the rest of their class; the Belfast lock-out of 1907 saw the independent Orange Order supporting the strike, a railway strike in the 1930's saw the IRA and Protestant trade unionists working together in agitational work. The Protestant community have and continue to produce a host of remarkable fighters against British rule in Ireland; the United Irishmen, Wolf Tone, Napper Tandy, Robert Emmet, Captain Jack White (military organiser of the Irish Citizen Army, one of the first workers militia's in Europe), Constance Markievicz the first women MP, for Sinn Fein, in Britain to name a few.

● The Fears of the Northern Irish Protestants

The Protestants, and many of the Catholics, in Northern Ireland see Southern Ireland as a backward and poor country; it's expensive to live in, controls unemployment by forcing its people to emigrate, it is a society that is dominated by the Roman Catholic church that makes access to abortion and contraception difficult and tries to enforce a miserable moral code on the working class. Welfare benefits are poor and health care is private and expensive. These are all good reasons not to want to enter into a united Ireland with the Southern State.

The Protestants fear being sold-out by the British ruling class, and as far as we can see they are quite right. Now that the economy of Northern Ireland is in tatters there is little economic reason for the British State to remain there. As was pointed out earlier the main reason for staying there is political; a withdrawal would destabilise the whole of Ireland with dangerous consequences for Europe and the rest of the capitalist system. Their long term aim is to 'stabilise' the situation and then pull out. If the Protestants get in the way of the British ruling class they will be sold down the river in just the same way as similar local groups were elsewhere in the Empire. The Protestants fear being overwhelmed by the Catholics. This has not happened to those Protestant communities in the three Ulster counties of Cavan, Monaghan and Donegal that were given to the South by the British. These communities were sold out because there was not enough Protestants in these counties to make it viable for them to keep political control. They have lived quite happily with their neighbours once removed from the influence of the Orange Order and the British State.

● The Protestants and the British

It is deeply ironic that although the Protestant Orange Order see themselves as British they are viewed as Irish by the British and as such are the target for all the usual bigotry and racism when they come to Britain.

● CLASS POLITICS AND NORTHERN IRELAND

In the present situation it is very difficult to engage in class struggle work in N. Ireland. The problem the working class face here is that they are in a colonial situation. It is hard to see how they are going to be able to move forward without ending the source of their division, colonialism itself as operated by the Orange elite and their British backers.

Not everyone in the Catholic areas is a Republican nor is every Protestant a Loyalist. Both parts of the class exist in a kind of siege, cut off from each other and the rest of their class in Ireland. The Republicans do however, as you might expect, look abroad and identify with similar struggles such as those of the Palestinians and the blacks in South Africa.

As in any colonial or imperialist situation the class war between the working class and the ruling class is distorted. It is not a straight fight. The working class faces various enemies at the same time.

The Protestant ruling class and their supporters in the working class are certainly part of the enemy. Those who carry out the orders of the ruling class and oppress the working class are also in the enemy camp; the RUC, UDR are protecting their own position as a privileged local group. The British Army squaddies in Ireland, most of whom don't know what the hell they are fighting for, are also in the enemy camp when they are 'doing their job' over there.

The reformist Social and Democratic Labour Party (SDLP) who will sell their grannies if they could do a deal with the British are also in the enemy camp. The Roman Catholic church with its woman hating dogma is also in the enemy camp. That just about leaves us with the Catholics and the Republicans and the unaligned Protestants (many do exist). The Catholic community are boxed in as we have just described. Every attempt to reach out to the Protestants has been met with brutal repression. They literally have only one choice; to continue resisting or go under.

The Republican movement is not one pure body, something that the British security forces will tell you. It is an alliance of different attitudes and classes and has changed over the years. Within each organisation are left, middle and right wings on the issue of class. The Irish National Liberation Army (INLA) and the Irish Republican Socialist Party (IRSP) were a more class struggle orientated group but have been damaged by feuds and splits, many believe with the assistance of the British security forces. There is a history of friction between Sinn Fein and the IRA. The situation is similar to what we expect to find in a revolutionary situation in Britain and elsewhere, a shifting set of political, military and social alliances.

‧The weakness of class politics in the Republican movement is for a number of reasons;

In the siege situation, split from the other half of the working class, there is great pressure to drop differences over class in order to pursue the immediate struggle to survive.

The effect of the Roman Catholic Church should not be under-estimated. It has its own plans for Ireland. Just like any other multinational company and the class war is not on its agenda!

The nationalist tradition lost much of its class content after the war with the British. It is this weakened tradition that the Catholics in the North have picked up.

The Left in Ireland and Britain failed the working class. Nowhere is this more evident than in Northern Ireland. Such failures are exposed in a crisis situation like that in Ireland and show what we too will face in a future revolution in Britain and elsewhere if we do not pursue our politics with the greatest energy now.

● IRELAND AND US

Although we think that Britain should stop meddling in Ireland our objective is not just a united Ireland. We are far more interested in a united Irish working class. Our objective is the destruction of capitalism, religion and the State, orange, green, pink or red.

● Reasons for Optimism

Even in such a desperate situation like Northern Ireland working class people still share experiences in common under capitalism. The Republican leadership have to add some measure of a socialist carrot to their rhetoric; ritual worship of James Connoly, the Irish socialist, is a must at most larger Republican events.

The bulk of the Northern Irish Catholic working class are committed to resisting the forces that represent the ruling classes, the IRA could not function otherwise. This however does not mean that support for the IRA or Sinn Fein etc. is unconditional or uncritical in the Catholic communities.

As the British ruling class pursues its plans for dumping the Orange elite and nibbling away at the privileges of the loyalists, the northern economy continues to slide into the pit. The use of the RUC against

Loyalist demonstrations in recent years, including the use of plastic bullets is a symptom of the slow success that the British are having at taming the Orange beast that was their own creation. Some of the dirty tricks campaign in Northern Ireland has been aimed at the Protestant elite as a part of this process e.g. the Kincora boys school scandal where senior Loyalists were implicated in a child-sex ring. The use of 'inquiries' into the RUC has been to scare them. The results were never going to be made public. It was to show what could be done, that British support was no longer unconditional. As a result the tensions set up in the RUC have been intense with a whole spate of suicides resulting from the stress. The Anglo-Irish agreement was another measure aimed at bringing the Unionists into line. There have been individuals in the Unionist organisations who have come to socialist conclusions but they have, to date, been killed or chucked out.

In the South of Ireland the population has something like 50% under the age of twenty-five. The power of the Roman Catholic church over the Irish youth is dropping rapidly. They are no longer entering the priesthood or convents. Things have got so bad that African priests are having to be sent to Ireland to plug the holes, reversing the historical place of the Irish in the African missions.

The southern economy is under the control of a small highly visible elite who are very publicly corrupt. The result for the Irish working class is one of the highest annual emigration rates in the world. Now with the world recession biting over the last few years, there is nowhere to go and many are coming back.

The possibilities for class struggle in the whole of Ireland are huge.

● The Irish Republicans and Us

We have to be clear about our attitude here, a situation like this is an acid-test of our politics. So far we have avoided going into the long list of atrocities and horrors that the British ruling class have inflicted on the Irish and continue to do so to this date. We do not intend to morally blackmail you into supporting the Republicans as do many of the British Left.

What is a problem however is the moralism that our ruling class plant in our heads. In their terms killing, torture and starvation are legitimate methods of pursuing their interests and is sanctioned by the State, explained by educationalists and blessed by the Church. For instance it is well known, and well documented, that undercover units

from the UDR, RUC, Army and SAS etc. have been involved in random sectarian killings, torture and the execution of Catholics and Republican activists. Yet we are told that it is only the IRA etc. that do this. We must not forget the scale of the propaganda war that the British State is waging over Northern Ireland, or that the main target of that war is us, the British working class.

Throughout the rest of the world Ireland is seen as suffering from British occupation and aggression. Ireland is seen as a war situation not a 'terrorist' problem caused by a few evil nutters, as we are told in the Britain.

When a group of people take on the superior organised might of the State and use force they have to use "all means necessary" as the black revolutionary Malcolm X pointed out. The only rules of war are that there are no rules except to kill the enemy, and World War One and Two, Vietnam and the Gulf War prove the point. There is no nice way to kill another human being. The outcry from the Left over the killing of three unarmed IRA volunteers in Gibraltar should be compared with a statement from the IRA on BBC radio;

"We understand the rules of war, all we ask is that you admit that your forces shot our volunteers on sight as we would expect to do to yours, and stop pretending otherwise."

During the Algerian war against the French, women and children were used to plant bombs. Criticised for this by the French, the Algerians replied "give us tanks and aeroplanes and we will gladly use them instead!" The French of course practised every conceivable barbarity in the pursuit of 'civilisation'.

Dreadful mistakes and the accidental killing of innocent people are what happens in war and we see no reason to believe that the coming class war between our class and our oppressors and enemies is going to be any different.

The Irish Republicans have made many mistakes and would be the first to agree. Some of these were plainly because of the lack of class politics, such as the Birmingham pub bombings where the enemy were seen as the English in general. Such actions are to say the least hard to explain or defend, except on the grounds of utter desperation. The more recent tactic of attacking military, political and economic targets is a more positive development.

As we pointed out in our general commentary on nationalism in Chapter Two we must remember that desperation often motivates those involved in anti-imperial struggles and this can be very difficult for many people to understand in a country like the UK. While we agree with the removal of such imperial and colonial oppression we argue and fight against the 'local' oppression waiting in the wings to take over the local management of capitalism.

James Connoly was dead clear about this difference between national liberation and the class war. On the eve of the 1916 rising during a lecture on the methods of guerilla war he advised the Irish Citizen Army as follows;

"If we should win, hold on to your rifles because the volunteers [nationalists] may have a different goal. Remember we're out not only for political liberty but for economic liberty as well. So hold on to your rifles."

It is worth repeating here our attitude to nationalism from Chapter One;

"What we must understand is that in the face of often brutal oppression nationalism gives working class people something. This

'something' is identity, pride, a feeling of community and solidarity and of course physical self-defence. We need to combat capitalism and its nationalism with something as strong i.e. - with our identity, pride, community, solidarity, history, culture and inspiration of the international working class's. To achieve this effectively will require courage, imagination and determination. To challenge nationalist ideas means doing more than saying that they are bad, we must prove that fighting for our class is better than fighting for a country."

In Northern Ireland the Republicans do try to attack what they consider legitimate targets; the security forces and those who work for them, economic targets, and members of Loyalist paramilitary groups. In contrast the security forces and Loyalist groups consider it OK to kill any Catholic as part of their policy of terrorising the whole community, and of course IRA members etc. when they can get them are also targets.

To say the IRA are responsible for dividing the working class in Northern Ireland would be about as sensible as blaming the blacks in South Africa for apartheid. The IRA are a symptom of a divided class and not the cause.

The British State has split and counter split the Irish people for the last 300 years. But the British ruling class has not had it all its own way over these years. Time and time again the Irish have united across the sectarian divide to drive out those who have used religious bigotry as a tool for ensuring Ireland is kept under direct rule from Britain.

Things will continue to become more and more difficult for the capitalists as the Irish working class realise that their interests are best served by uniting across the sectarian divide to smash not only capitalism but all those who have helped perpetuate direct rule from Britain.

We do support the struggle against the British State in Northern Ireland as we support all working class people fighting against oppression and look forward to the removal of British domination. We do not give uncritical support to any nationalist organisation.

We look forward to the struggle against oppresion being widened in Ireland to include that against capitalism, both British and Irish, and the Catholic and Protestant churches. We also greatly look forward to the Protestant working class regaining its proud older tradition of unity with the rest of their class against oppression from both outside Ireland and within.

● What Can We Do To Hasten These Things?

Educate ourselves out of the abysmal ignorance, complacency and arrogance about Ireland that the media encourage in us.

By continuing to agitate and inform our class we can make as much trouble for the British ruling class as possible. The best way to help those struggling against British imperialism in Ireland is to step up the class war against the British ruling class at home. Lenin said this and it just goes to show you can't be wrong all the time!

Raise the issue of Ireland in our class in the same way we do with other issues.

To the best of our abilities encourage the development of our kind of approach to class politics in Ireland, North and South. *AFTER ALL WE ARE INTERNATIONALISTS.*

Marx

Having mentioned the name of Marx this is the place to comment on his ideas. At the time of his writing the dominant ideas concerning capitalism and the organisation of society were, not surprisingly, those of the ruling class. 'Thinkers' like Bentham, Smith and Locke were used to justify and explain the introduction of capitalism, whether they were really into it is another matter.

Marx set himself the task of attacking these ideas head-on at their own level, that of academic economics and philosophy. This together with the fact that he was writing in German over 100 years ago does not make him an easy read! What he was up against were ideas that are still dominant today. They are usually attributed to the economist Adam Smith. They go something like this; in capitalism there are three elements - land (physical resources), labour and capital.

The capitalist brings these together to produce something which he then sells on the market for a profit. The value and hence profit of making an item is determined solely by the market and that market is governed by 'market forces', i.e. brutal competition. In this version of the world the capitalist is the central player and labour: the working class, is relegated to the role of another item of production like land. You don't have to be a genius to see that labour gets the shit end of the stick in this set up.

Nevertheless this was, and is, roughly the way the ruling class viewed the world and it gave them the 'right' to do as they pleased. The fact is they really believe all this. After all, if nobody tells you different you will never change your mind. The egotism of these people is that they think that they are the centre of the world and their power certainly feeds this illusion.

Marx sought to challenge this outlook by trying to explain capitalism on another basis. He made labour the central element in his theory of capitalist economics and tried to prove that 'value' and hence profit was determined solely by the amount of work put into creating it. This had the effect of switching the foundation of capitalism away from the capitalist class to the working class. The intention was to prove that the workers could do without the capitalists but not vice-versa. The aim of all this was to show that the capitalist far from being a gift to the human race were, in effect, a bunch of parasites who should be got rid of. Of course Marx had a lot of other ideas too and incorporated a lot of other peoples work in his writing.

To an extent Marx was correct in his efforts. Labour is crucial to creating wealth and profit. Without our labour capitalism will grind to a halt. But that's about all you can say. Marx's "Labour Theory of Value" tried to show how value was exactly determined by labour. His eagerness to try and show this in a precise scientific way has to be understood in the light of his times;

The 19th century was a time when 'science' was all the rage and academic people believed the scientific approach would unlock everything. Marx was into this fashion and applied it to the problem of value and profit, hence his use of obscure methods and formulae.

He believed if he could 'crack' the problem of value and show that it was dependent on labour and not the market then he would have the basis of a philosophy that could destroy capitalism.

Finally he was a Liberal, although this is in the 19th century sense of the word, and felt the need to justify the right of the working class to

the wealth of society.

We have to acknowledge the achievements of the man as did his contemporaries in the anarchist movement like Bakunin. Ideas such as;

"Historical Materialism" - the way of looking at history from the point of view of the economic forces at work is a really useful tool. (Marx took the work of a German, Hegel, and developed it).

The man's appreciation of the relation between the economic workings of a society and its political and cultural life (or as he put it the relation between the 'base' and the 'superstructure').

Marx's use of 'dialectics' to tie all this together was a real achievement and a real pain in the arse to read! Dialectics is the art of incorporating elements of opposing arguments together to reach a position of greater truth or knowledge or, if you like, an appreciation of the to and fro of events and history. But, Marx did place great emphasis on capitalism behaving according to its own internal laws and tended to believe it would ultimately destroy itself. We do not agree with this or his plans for change concerning the beneficial role of the State. Marx was a politician as well as an economist and philosopher and understood some of the criticisms made of him and like a good academic "covered his back". He did this by using his skill in dialectics to block counter-arguments by anticipating them and incorporating their ideas into his own theory. Thus reading Marx is very difficult not just because he was a high flying academic who deliberately bent the meaning of words, in German, a 100 years ago. He has also placed loads of his 'dialectical road-blocks' on the paths to understanding and criticising his writings.

Not surprisingly, then, over the last 100 years people have been able to read all sorts of things into Marx, rather like the Bible! We should look at the useful things he has to give us rather than get into a sterile debate about what he 'really' meant, because we should know what we 'really' want. Depending on what bit of Marx you read, from what bit of his career, you may end up with a contradictory set of ideas. For instance his very early writing is a lot more humanist than his later writing which concentrates on economics.

There is evidence that Marx re-thought some of his ideas later in life, particularly after the crushing of the Paris commune in 1871, and came to conclusions that criticised his own work including parts of the communist manifesto that stressed the positive role the State had to play. No mention of Marx seems to be proper without the obligatory quotes. Here he seems to have changed his tune on the role of the State compared to his writing in the communist manifesto;

"The working class cannot simply lay hold on the ready-made State machinery and wield it for their own purpose. The political instrument of their enslavement cannot serve as the political instrument of their emancipation".

"It is a revolution against the State itself, of this supernaturalist abortion of a society, a resumption by the people for the people of its own social life. It is not a revolution to transfer it from one faction of the ruling class to another, but a revolution to break down this horrid machinery of class domination itself."

- from a draft copy of "The Civil War In France" - 1871.

The great money trick

Taken from "The Ragged Trousered Philanthropist" - by Robert Tressel.

"**Money is the** real cause of poverty," said Owen.

"Prove it," repeated Crass.

"Money is the cause of poverty because it is the device by which those who are too lazy to work are enabled to rob the workers of the fruits of their labour."

"Prove it," said Crass.

Owen slowly folded up the piece of newspaper he had been reading and put it into his pocket.

"All right," he replied. "I'll show you how the Great Money Trick is worked."

Owen opened his dinner basket and took from it two slices of bread, but as these were not sufficient, he requested that anyone who had some bread left should give it to him. They gave him several pieces, which he placed in a heap on a clean piece of paper, and, having borrowed the pocket knives they used to cut and eat their dinners with from Easton, Harlow and Philpot, he addressed them as follows:

"These pieces of bread represent the raw materials which exist naturally in and on the earth for the use of mankind; they were not made by any human being, but were created for the benefit and sustenance of all, the same as were the air and the light of the sun."

"Now," continued Owen, "I am a capitalist; or rather, I represent the landlord and capitalist class. That is to say, all these raw materials belong to me. It does not matter for our present argument how I obtained possession of them; the only thing that matters now is the admitted fact that all the raw materials which are necessary for the production of the necessaries of life are now the property of the landlord and capitalist class. I am that class: all these raw materials belong to me."

"Now you three represent the working class. You have nothing, and for my part, although I have these raw materials, they are of no use to me. What I need is the things that can be made out of these raw materials by work: but I am too lazy to work for me. But first I must explain that I possess something else beside the raw materials. These three knives represent all the machinery of production; the factories, tools, railways, and so forth, without which the necessaries of life cannot be produced in abundance. And these three coins" - taking three half pennies from his pocket - "represent my money, capital."

"But before we go any further," said Owen, interrupting himself, "it is important that you remember that I am not supposed to be merely a capitalist. I represent the whole capitalist class. You are not supposed to be just three workers, you represent the whole working class."

Owen proceeded to cut up one of the slices of bread into a number of little square blocks.

"These represent the things which are produced by labour, aided by machinery, from the raw materials. We will suppose that three of these blocks represent a week's work. We will suppose that a week's work is worth one pound."

Owen now addressed himself to the working classes as represented by Philpot, Harlow and Easton.

"You say that you are all in need of employment, and as I am the kind-hearted capitalist class I am going to invest all my money in

Hand over the BREAD!

various industries, so as to give you plenty of work. I shall pay each of you one pound per week, and a week's work is that you must each produce three of these square blocks. For doing this work you will each receive your wages; the money will be your own, to do as you like with, and the things you produce will of course be mine, to do as I like with. You will each take one of these machines and as soon as you have done a week's work, you shall have your money."

The working classes accordingly set to work, and the capitalist class sat down and watched them. As soon as they had finished, they passed the nine little blocks to Owen, who placed them on a piece of paper by his side and paid the workers their wages.

"These blocks represent the necessaries of life. You can't live without some of these things, but as they belong to me, you will have to buy them from me: my price for these blocks is, one pound each."

As the working classes were in need of the necessaries of life and as they could not eat, drink or wear the useless money, they were compelled to agree to the kind capitalist's terms. They each bought back, and at once consumed, one-third of the produce of their labour. The capitalist class also devoured two of the square blocks, and so the net result of the week's work was that the kind capitalist had consumed two pounds worth of the things produced by the labour of the others, and reckoning the squares at their market value of one pound each, he had more than doubled his capital, for he still possessed the three pounds is money and in addition four pounds worth of goods. As for the working classes, Philpot, Harlow and Easton, having each consumed the pound's worth of necessaries they had bought with their wages, they were again in precisely the same condition as when they started work - they had nothing.

This process was repeated several times: for each week's work the producers were paid their wages. They kept on working and spending all their earnings. The kind-hearted capitalist consumed twice as much as any one of them and his pool of wealth continually increased. In a little while, reckoning the little squares at their market value of one pound each, he was worth about one hundred pounds, and the working classes were still in the same condition as when they began, and were still tearing into their work as if their lives depended upon it.

After a while the rest of the crowd began to laugh, and their merriment increased when the kind-hearted capitalist, just after having sold a pound's worth of necessaries to each of his workers, suddenly took their tools, the machinery of production, the knives, away from them, and informed them that as owing to over production all his store-housed were glutted with the necessaries of life, he had decided to close down the works.

"Well, and wot the bloody 'ell are we to do now?" Demanded Philpot.

"That's not my business," replied the kind-hearted capitalist. "I've paid your wages, and provided you with plenty of work for a long time past. I have no more work for you to do at present. Come round again in a few months' time and I'll see what I can do for you."

"But what about the necessaries of life?" Demanded Harlow.

"We must have something to eat."

"Of course you must," replied the capitalist, affably; "and I shall be very pleased to sell you some."

"But we ain't got no bloody money!"

"Well, you can't expect me to give you my goods for nothing! You didn't work for me for nothing, you know. I paid you for you work and you should have saved something: you should have been thrifty like me. Look how I have got on by being thrifty!"

The unemployed looked blankly at each other, but the rest of the crowd only laughed; and then the three unemployed began to abuse the kind-hearted capitalist, demanding that he should give them some of the necessaries of life that he had piled up in his warehouses, or to be allowed to work and produce some more for their own needs; and even threatened to take some of the things by force if he did not comply with their demands. But the kind-hearted capitalist told them not to be insolent, and spoke to them about honesty, and said if they were not careful he would have their faces battered in for them by the police, or if necessary he would call out the military and have them shot down like dogs, the same as he had done before at Featherstone and Belfast.

A short history of the class war federation

The Class War Federation emerged from the wreckage of the British anarchist and Left political scene of the 1980's. At that time many of the groups and individuals making up that scene, apart from a few exceptions, were retreating from class struggle into reformism or obscure and elitist middle class substitutes. It was not a pretty sight. Many of the anarchists became involved in a mishmash of single issue politics, middle class moral outrage and fashion! The Left on the other hand were busy trying to protect what party structures they had left and setting about reconstructing "the new politics of socialism" - where the working class had either ceased to exist or were no longer important. Our early years were partly a reaction against this sickening spectacle.

The miners strike of 1984/5 was a turning point for many of those in the anarchist scene. The reality of class struggle was forced upon them. Sales of our paper *Class War* soared as we took a no nonsense line about violence in the strike. Eventually a federation was formed which had a simple set of aims and principles that stressed the importance of class struggle. Some people could not accept the idea of such a degree of organisation and left. For a considerable period each issue of the paper was produced in rotation by different groups around the country; a fairly unique approach in the Left. The early years of the Federation, then, were spent producing populist propaganda and staging publicity stunts like 'Bash the Rich' marches, the 'Mug a Yuppie' campaign, national 'Wreck a Roller Day', disrupting the Henley Regatta and other upper class do's. All with varying degrees of success. We also spent a fair amount of time arguing and debating with the Left and anarchist groups.

While there are many fine people in the Left and anarchist movement in the UK, there are also those who are not so fine. Of this latter group we attracted our fair share. Over a period of time these people were either 'cured' or chucked out, sometimes both! We quickly learned a lot about people and ourselves in the process. This was also a period of great internal debate about methods of organisation, something which anarchists are always, and rightly, concerned about. It was during this whole process of growing and learning that it gradually became clear to us that little more was to be gained by

bothering about or arguing with the Left or anarchist scene in the UK. The best course seemed to be to go our own way and just get on with what we were doing. This, as it turned out, was the correct decision. We were freed from the historical obstruction that both movements had become. We just went around them. This is still our strategy today.

We carried on with our popular approach to class politics and got better at turning the enemies propaganda weapons back at them. To our pleasure we were getting more and more positive feedback from the working class heartland: the council estates, the prisons, the armed forces, youth clubs, factories, etc. Our mailbag was, and is, more interesting than that of the established Left. People began to take more and more bulk orders of papers to sell to friends. It quickly became clear that the readership of the paper was far higher than its actual sales, encouraging as these were. The paper was, and is, passed from hand to hand and our flyposters and stickers have become collectors items with people begging for them as we paste them up! A situation unique in the recent history of the Left.

Our national "Rock Against The Rich" concert tour with ex-Clash singer Joe Strummer was a great success in every way except financially. Well, we nearly broke even! The tour spread the name and basic message of Class War far and wide and proved that class politics can also mean having a good time. The production of the paper was eventually centralised in one location for economic and practical reasons, with writers and editors spread all over the country. The paper, we believe, has got better and better. Interestingly enough the paper is entirely self-financing, something quite unique in the British Left. To help us keep it that way you will find a form at the back of this book for a subscription and other Class War goodies! The paper is sold on the street, at football matches, in newsagents, record shops and at concerts etc.

We also produce a theoretical discussion magazine called "*The Heavy Stuff*", where individual members and supporters contribute articles to provoke discussion. This magazine is quickly becoming a collectors item. On the international front the Federation is in touch with like-minded groups all around the world. Our ambition is to be a part of a growing international working class movement that can change this world. To this end we held a highly successful international conference in London in September 1991.

The Federation came to prominence after the 1990 poll tax riot in Trafalgar square where the Metropolitan Police got a well deserved beating at the hands of working class people from all over the country. One of our representatives, when interviewed on TV, was asked to condemn the rioters behaviour, he refused and praised those involved as working class heroes. The media was gob-smacked, questions were asked in parliament and parts of our publications read out in the House of Commons and the Lords. A representative of a left-wing party called Militant, you may remember them, was asked the same question by the media. He not only condemned the rioters but offered to name them to the police. Nothing could have illustrated more starkly the difference between our approach and politics and those of the Left.

Our direct, hard-hitting approach also caused no end of worrying in Whitehall when during the 1992 General Election campaign the Anti-Election Alliance, in which the Federation played a major role, was banned from holding a march and rally in Central London. In reply we told them what they could do with their ban, and with just days to go they backed down. On the day, the 1500 participants were shadowed by a huge force of over 3500 police, who, according to *Police Review* magazine were specially drafted in from all over South East England. But, surprise surprise, this event with its resulting massive police mobilisation, coming just days before the vote was taken, was subject to a complete press blackout. The silence was deafening!

● How the Class War Federation Works

We work on a federal system, each group and individual members come together to achieve commonly agreed objectives. The Federation is a membership organisation with membership fees and certain obligations, such as the understanding and promotion of the Federation's politics and propaganda. We have a simple constitution and members are expected to abide by it. Federalism is a method of organising that provides a large degree of freedom for members and groups within a broadly agreed set of politics and strategy *(for a fuller description and discussion of federalism see Chapter Seven)*.

When the Federation as a whole takes decisions affecting the whole membership, such as adopting a particular strategy, members are expected to comply. If they do not they are free to leave; we are not dreamy liberals. Members and groups either represent themselves or send delegates to represent them at Federation meetings. All delegates are instantly re-callable by those whom they represent and are directly accountable to them.

Nobody occupies a permanent post within the Federation. The positions such as secretaries, editors, organisers, treasurers etc. are open to election at least twice a year at our national conference. This national conference is the prime decision making body of the Federation. Between conferences the day to day business is handled by a regular meeting of the National Delegate Committee. The Federation also holds weekend schools for discussion and education.

The Federation is divided into geographic regions where the groups and members are encouraged to form their own regional organisation with their own campaigns, weekend schools, conferences, internal bulletins etc. As you can see the emphasis in our way of organising is on members and groups acting under their own steam as much as possible. The central control of the Left is neither politically healthy or indeed capable of waging the struggle required to help form a working class movement that will destroy capitalism.

● The Future

Whether the Federation prospers or fails will depend on its members and external events, but we do think our approach and basic ideas are correct. Just as importantly we think that the spirit in which we work is very important and believe we have retrieved the older tradition that the Left has lost. We do not claim perfection, we have made mistakes in the past, and learnt from them, and shall probably make mistakes in the future, that's what happens in the real world.

Some of these books and pamphlets may only be available from anarchist and left-wing bookshops and publishers. The title of the book is followed by the authors name and the publisher (if shown).

● RECOMMENDED

"Albions Fatal Tree". Douglas and Thompson.

"World Turned Upside Down". Christopher Hill.

"The Making of the English Working Class". E.P. Thompson.

"The Great Arch". Corrigan and Sayer.

"The Eclipse and Re-emergence of the Communist Movement". Barrot and Martin.

"Harry McShane (no mean fighter)". Harry McShane and Joan Smith.

"The History of the Makhovist Movement". Peter Arshinov.

"The Black Jacobins". C.L.R. James.

"The Making of the Irish Working Class". Peter Berresford Ellis.

"The Ragged Trousered Philanthropist". Robert Tressel.

"Dynamite! (A century of class struggle in America, 1830 - 1930)". Lewis Adamic - Rebel Press.

"The Platform of the Libertarian Communists". Reprinted by Workers Solidarity Movement, Ireland.

"Anarchy". Errico Maltesta - Freedom Press.

"Strange Victories" (A criticism of the anti-nuclear and environmental movements). Elephant Editions.

"Heroes". John Pilger.

● GENERAL

"The Tyranny of Structurelessness". Jo Freeman - Raven Press.

"A Critique of State Socialism". Michael Bakunin.

"The Retreat from Class; the 'new' socialism". Ellen Meiksins Wood - Verso.

"Mutinies". David Lamb - Solidarity Press.

"Krondstat". Ida Mett.

"Love and Rage". Carl Harp.

"The Willhemshaven Uprising". Icarus.

"Zapata". Penfold.

"The Invergordon Mutineer". Len Wincott - Freedom Press.

"The Communist Manifesto". Marx and Engels.

"Labour Theory of Value". Marx and Engels.

"Beneath the City Streets". Peter Laurie.

"Divided Kingdom". John Osmond - Channel 4 Books.

"The History and Practice of the Political Police in Britain". Tony Bunyan.

"The Technology of Political Control". Carol Ackroyd.

"The Uses of Literacy". Richard Hoggart.

"Petals of Blood". Ngugi Wa Thiong'o.

"Homage To Catalonia". George Orwell.

"Hungary 1956". Andy Anderson.

"Sabotage". Geoff Brown.

"Marxist Economics for Socialists". John Harrison - *Militant* publications.

"Spartacus". James Leslie Mitchell.

"How Socialist is the Socialist Workers Party". A Wildcat pamphlet.

"Anarchy, from Loyalism to Anarchism". J.R. White - Cienfuegos Press.

"Capitalism and its Revolutionary Destruction". A Wildcat pamphlet.

"A Critique of Marxism". Sam Dolgoff - Soil of Liberty Press (USA).

"Chile: the Guerillas Are Amongst Us". Helio Prieto - Pluto Press.

"Paper Boys. Accounts of picketing at Wapping". Booklet produced by printers involved in the News International strike.

"Poll Tax Riot, 10 hours that shook Trafalgar Square". ACAB Press.

"Malatestas life and Ideas". Freedom Press.

"Deterring Democracy". Noam Chomsky - Verso.

"What is Communist Anarchism?". Alexander Berkman.

"The Slow Burning Fuse; the Lost History of the British Anarchists". J. Quail.

"The Irrational in Politics". Solidarity.

"God and the State". Michael Bakunin.

"The Reproduction of Everyday Life". Fredy Perlman - Black and Red Books.

"Bad News", "Really Bad News", "Very Bad News". Glasgow University media group.

"Sabate - Guerilla Extraordinary". Antonio Tellez

"How it all Began". Willie Bauman - Pulp Press (USA).

"Bury My Heart at Wounded Knee". Dee Brown.

"The Iron Heel". Jack London.

"City Within a State: a Portrait of Britains Financial World". Anthony Hilton.

"Capital City". Hamish McRae.

"The Menace of Fascism". Ted Grant - *Militant* Publications.

"Fighting the Revolution". Freedom Press.

"From Riot to Insurrection". Alfred M. Bonanno - Elephant Editions.

"Media, State and Nation". Phillip Schlesinger - Sage.

"Out of the Ghetto". Joe Jacobs - Phoenix Press.

"Breaking Free". Attack International.

"The Free". Hooligan Press.

"The Bonnot Gang". Richard Parry - Rebel Press.

"Failure of a Revolution". Sebastian Hafner.

"British Syndicalism". Bob Holton - Pluto Press.

"Poland '80-'82". Henri Simon - Black and Red.

"Revolutionary Hamburg". Richard A. Comfort - Stamford University Press.

"Durruti, The People Armed". Abel Paz - Black Rose Books.

"The Spanish Revolution". Burnette Bolleton - Chapel Hill.

"Reading Capital Politically". Harry Cleaver - Harvester Press.

"Lenin - Selected Works". Lenin.

"Capital 1 - 3". Marx.

"Revolt on the Clyde". William Gallagher - Lawrence and Wishart.

"The Bolsheviks and Workers Control". Maurice Brinton - Black and Red.

"Revolution and Counter Revolution in Spain". Felix Morron - Pathfinder.

"Red Petrograd". S.A. Smith - Cambridge University Press.

"State Capitalism and World Revolution". C.L.R. James - Charles H. Kerr.

"A Peoples History of the United States". Howard Zinn - Harper and Row.

"Bakunin on Anarchism". Bakunin - Black Rose Books.

"The Paris Commune". Lissagary - New Park.

"A Peoples History of England". Al Morton - Lawrence and Wishart.

"Ten Days That Shook the World". John Reed - Penguin.

"Lucy Parsons, American Revolutionary". Carolyn Ashbaugh - Charles H. Kerr.

"Collectives in the Spanish Revolution". Gaston Leval - Freedom Press.

"Pannekoek and the Workers Councils". Serge Bricianar - Telos Press.

"Anarchism". Daniel Guerin - Monthly Review Press.

"Birth of our Power". Victor Serge - Writers and Readers.

"The Chomsky Reader". Noam Chomsky - Serpents Tail.

"The Spanish Cockpit". Franz Borkenau.

"Reform or Revolution?". Rosa Luxemburg.

"Lessons of the Spanish Revolution". Freedom Press.

"The Tragedy of Spain". Rudolph Rocker.

● IRISH BOOKLIST

"Spirit of Freedom". Attack International.

"Ireland: the Propaganda War". Liz Curtiz - Pluto Press.

"On Another Man's Wound", "The Singing Flame". Ernie O'Malley.

"The Longest War". Kevin Kelley - Brandon Zed.

"The Crack". Sally Belfrage - Grafton.

"Only the Rivers Run Free". E. Fairweather, R. McDonald & M. McFadyean.

"Twenty Years On". Micheal Farrell - Brandon.

"War and an Irish Town". Eamon Mcann - Pluto Press.

"Out of the Maze". Derek Dunne - Gill and Macmillan.

"Ten Dead Men". David Beresford - Grafton.

"The Irish Civil War". Frances Blake - Information on Ireland.

"One Day In My Life". Bobby Sands - Pluto Press.

"Trinity". Leon Uris - Grafton.

● SCOTTISH BOOKLIST

"The Lion in the North", "The Highland Clearances", "Darien Disaster", "Mutiny in the Highland Regiments", "Glencoe". John Prebble.

"Scotland: A Concise History". James Halliday - Gordon Wright.

"Scotland at the Crossroads". James Young - Clydeside Press.

"John Maclean: His Life and Times". Graham Bain - John Maclean Society.

"John Maclean". Nan Milton.

"Dictionary of Scottish History". Gordon Donaldson.

"Rousing of the Scottish Working Class". James Young.

"Tartans". Christian Hesketh.

"Scottish Womens Suffrage Movement". Elspeth King.

"A Short History of Labour in Scotland". W.H. Marwick.

"The Language of the People". William Donaldson.

"The Strike of the Glasgow Weavers 1787". Elspeth King.

"The Scottish Insurrection of 1820". Peter Berresford Ellis and Seumas Mac.

"A'Ghobhain". Pluto Press.

"Conflict and Class 1700 - 1838". Hamish Fraser - John Donald.

"The Making of the Crofting Community". James Hunter - John Donald.

"The Struggle for a Language". Gwen Mulholland - Rank and File Teacher.

"Glasgow: Going for a Song". Sean Demer - Lawrence and Wishart.

"Glasgow: The Uneasy Truce". Tom Gallagher - Manchester University Press.

"Workers City: The Real Glasgow Stands Up", "The Reckoning: Beyond the Culture City Rip Off". Farquhar Maclay - Clydeside Press.

"Voices From Scotlands' Recent Past". Billy Key - Polygon.

● WELSH BOOKLIST

"When Was Wales?". Gwyn A. Williams - Penguin.

"Insurrection in Wales". D. Helen Allday - Terence Dalton.

"Before Rebecca". David Jones - Penguin.

"The Rebecca Riots". Christopher Schest - Longmans.

"The Merthyr Rising". Glyn A. Williams - Crook Helm.

"Political Policing in Wales". Welsh Campaign for Civil and Political Liberties.

"Police Conspiracy". John Osmond - Y Lolfa.

"Miners Against Fascism". Lawrence and Wishart.

"The Welsh Extremist". Ned Thomas - Y Lolfa.

"Turning to London". Robert Griffiths - Welsh Socialist Party.

"Get Off Our Backs: Wales a Colony". Tim Richards - Welsh Socialist Party.

"A People and a Proletariat - Essays in the History of Wales". Dai Smith - Pluto Press.

Class War Federation

Class War Supporters

If you want to find out more about the Class War Federation, about its politics, internal workings, organisation and membership, then this is a must for you.

In the supporter's Bulletin, you will find news ,views, decisions, updates and debates on whats happening in and around the Federation. Find out how you can be involved with whats happening in your area and the rest of the country.

To subscribe, just photocopy the form below. It costs just £1.50 for six months, and gives you three bulletins in that time. Don't wait apply now and support Britains fastest growing, dynamic revolutionary organisation.

Supporters Bulletin

NAME_____

ADDRESS_____

_____

I enclose £1.50 cheque/postal order payable to 'Class War'

Here's an extra donation for £......

Send to: SUPPORTERS' SEC, PO BOX 2027 REDDITCH, 898 ONT

Class War is active in most towns and cities across Britain. If you want to get involved in your area please photocopy the form below and we will put you in touch with your local Regional Secretary, who will let you know more about the Federation and how we opperate.

Membership form

NAME_____

ADDRESS_____

_____

Fill out and return this form, and your local organiser will contact you about becoming a member.
Send to:MEMBERSHIP SEC', PO BOX 467 LONDON, E8 3QX

The Paper

Class War 'Britains most unruly tabloid', hits the streets every six weeks, packed with up to date, hard hitting news and views. To ensure you get your copy, subscribe now, by photocopying this form and sending it off to us......

PAPER SUBSCRIPTION

please send me the next
- ☐ turbo sub(£10.00)
- ☐ 12 issues(£5.00)
- ☐ 6 issues(£2.50)

NAME_____

ADDRESS_____

_____

Send cheque/postal order payable to 'Class War', to C.W, PO BOX 772, Bristol, BS99 1EG.

The Heavy Stuff

The Heavy Stuff is Class Wars' theoretical/ discussion magazine, 'the thought behind the anger'.

HEAVY STUFF SUBSCRIPTION

- ☐ £6.00 for 4 issues

NAME_____

ADDRESS_____

_____

Send cheque/ postal order payable to 'Heavy Stuff', to PO BOX 1QF, Newcastle-U-Tyne, NE 99 1QF

Class War :A Decade of Disorder

ISBN 0 86091 5581
£8.00

for a blast from the past, this 130 page book looks at some of the best (and worst!) articles, pictures,and graphics from the first fifty editions of CLASS WAR.

Decade of Disorder is available to the trade and for mailorder from A.K. Distribution, 3, Balmoral Place, Stirling, Scotland. FK8 2RD

AK PRESS

3 BALMORAL PLACE

STIRLING

SCOTLAND

FK 8 2 RD

For a catalogue of all the several thousands of other books, magazines and pamphlets; on anarchism, feminism, history, philosophy etc, fiction and non-fiction, from fanzines to graphic novels send a LARGE SAE to the address above.

Poll Tax Rebellion is the gripping inside story of the biggest mass movement in British history, one of which at its peak involved over 17 million people. Using a combination of photos, text and graphics it's a thrilling celebration of our power from Trafalgar Square to the fall of Thatcher.

Drawing on the voices of activists and non-payers, it describes the everyday organisation of the local Anti-Poll Tax Unions. It chronicles in detail the demonstrations and riots of March 1990, culminating in the massive battle of Trafalgar. It shows how the courts were blocked, the bailiffs resisted and the Poll Tax, in its origional form, destroyed. The final chapter draws on our experiences to present a radically new vision of change from below.
Copies available from
A.K. Press £4.95,
ISBN 1 873176 50 3

Further A.K Press Titles

Terrorising The Neighbourhood

American Foreign Policy in the Post-Cold War Era

Noam Chomsky

ISBN 1 873176 00 7
£3.95 + 64p pp

Traces the origins, goals and implications of U.S foreign policy in recent years. The book explores the way in which the White House secures the worlds wealth for the entrenched elites that own and run the United states. A vivid introduction to both the New World Order, and the work of a major theorist, the text vindicates Chomsky's long held position on foreign intervention.

The Bigger Tory Vote

The Covert Sequestration of the Bigotry Vote

Nick Toczek

ISBN 1 873176 20 1
£2.95 + 48p pp

Investigates the absorbtion of neo-fascist, racist and other far right elements into the Conservative Party since the late 1940s

The Assult On Culture

Utopian Currents from
Lettrisme to Class War

Stewart Home
ISBN 1 873176 30 9
£5.95 + £1.28 pp

A brief introduction to a vast array of political and artistic oppo-
nents to the dominant culture. "A
concise introduction to a whole
mess of troublemakers through
the ages...well-written, incisive
and colourful." (N.M.E.)

On The Mass Bombing Of Iraq and Kuwait

or Leonard's Shorter cat-
echism

Tom Leonard
ISBN 1 873176 25 2
£1.95 + 26p pp

A series of saterical questions
and answers on the Gulf War
and its aftermath by the cel-
ebrated Scots poet; with a pref-
ace in which he examines the
role of the media in reporting the
war.

Sabotage in the American Workplace

Edited by
Martin Sprouse,
illustrated by Tracey Cox
ISBN 1 873176 65 1
£9.95

Sabotage in the workplace is as common as work itself. This book consists of 250 anecdotes from employees at all levels of the American workforce- blue collar to white collar, government agencies and the private sector, autoworkers, bus-drivers, paramedics, soldiers, prostitutes, secretaries, postal-workers, stock-brokers, lawyers, paperboys....tell how, by taking matters into their own hands they have gotten back at the bosses. Wether because of boredom, harrassment, poor working conditions, low pay or ethics, they have joined self empowerment. From slacking off to computer logic bombs, petty theft to the destruction of heavy equipment, sabotage is everywhere!